How to Catch the Big Idea

THE STRATEGIES OF THE TOP-CREATIVES

RALF LANGWOST

Bibliographic information published by Die Deutsche Bibliothek
Die Deutsche Bibliothek lists this publication in the Deutsche Nationalbibliografie;
detailed bibliographic data is available in the Internet at http://dnb.ddb.de

Translated from the German by Kim Butcher and Denis Buckley

ISBN 3-89578-238-6

http://www.publicis-erlangen.de/books

Editor: IdeaManagement® Institut für top-kreatives Prozess-Design, Frankfurt/Main
Publisher: Publicis Corporate Publishing, Erlangen
© 2004 by Publicis KommunikationsAgentur GmbH, GWA, Erlangen

Printed in Germany

IDEAMANAGEMENT®

PUBLICIS

Dedicated to The Creative Spirit and its Children

Dan: »*Some days you go fishing and there's nothing out there, is that your fault? Maybe, maybe not, but the conscious mind is not the only thing involved in the creation of good work.*«

Don: »*It's a little bit like fishing, waiting, talking, having a beer and that thing, you know there's something there, you know you have got something that day, it's real. It's a little like fishing, it's like getting a tug from somewhere down in there.*«

Dan: »*It's just like fishing, you just start writing, it's like free association, it's like Hemingway sharpening pencils or something.*«

Preface

The two questions I get asked most often regarding creativity.

'Where do you get your ideas from' and, 'When do you do your best thinking?'

The answer to the first question is 'if I knew, I'd spend a lot more time there.' And to the second, 'when I'm not thinking.'

If both those answers seem a bit glib, I apologise. I don't mean them to be. Except to illustrate the point that having ideas is a bit of a mystery.

I think it's one of the most wonderful things we all do. And I emphasise all, because everyone has ideas. Some maybe better than others and some more profound. But essentially we all do it. It isn't the preserve of a few. In fact the painter Joseph Beuys said, 'we're all artists, but not everyone should exhibit.'

What makes having ideas in business so incredible is you are creating something from nothing. It needs nothing more than your imagination, a pencil maybe and possibly a pad. That's it. And with those simple tools, you can change the fortunes of industries.

It is at the very core of human development. Without it we would be nothing.

Everyone I know has their own 'formula' for how they do it. The checks, the balances, the stimuli and most of all dealing with the dreaded creative block.

Hopefully this book will help you unblock those barriers and get your creative juices flowing.

As I have learned over the years, when it comes to having ideas, I'll try almost anything to make them better.

John Hegarty, BBH, London

Contents

Thank You

This book is the second stage of a research project, which examines the Strategies of Top-Creatives. It condenses, expands and deepens into the knowledge arising from interviews with 77 international Top-Creatives. This only became possible through the commitment and openness with which many people have contributed their knowledge. I thank you with all my heart.

Birgit Hüther, Hans Lauber, Claudia Strixner, Michael Wölfle for the trust and support of MGM, Mediagruppe München, who promoted the project financially.

Michael Conrad, Ex CCO of Leo Burnett, Chicago, who as President of the Jury enthused several other Creatives from all parts of the world spontaneously for the project and already promised me his support at the Cannes Advertising Film Festival in 1996. Thanks also goes to Donald Gunn (Gunn Report, London) and Walter Petersen (Leo Burnett, Chicago); Pieter van Velsen (Lowe Kuiper Schouten, Amsterdam); John R. Fawcett (previously Bates Worldwide, Sydney/New York); Hansjörg Zürcher (Advico Young&Rubicam, Zurich).

Particular thanks also goes to Julia Crompton for her untiring dedication as camera woman, secretary, translator and project manager between Hawaii und Prague, Prof. Dr. Werner Gaede from the Universität der Künste in Berlin, who inspired me as my professor and who was my mentor for the project. Prof. Harald Pulch from the Fachhochschule Mainz. Harald Gasper for his support in the development of the questionnaire. André Kemper, for making himself available for the prototype-test for the interview method. Klaus Marwitz for the German Nautilus-Version on personality analysis. Charly Mayr for the compilation of the databank template, Phyllis-Renée Boldt, Petra Harms, Juan Carlos Alarcón Mendoza for the reliable input into the databank. Jeanette Histed and Simone Wilms for the transcription of the interviews.

I would like to thank Tatjana Gravenstein for the inspiring design of the book in all of its phases and her dedicated support, Jérôme Müller for the front picture, Lisa Schulze-Oechtering for the fine-tuning of the layout and Sylvia Kasmer for the office support.

Thank you to Gerhard Seitfudem and Publicis Corporate Publishing for the dedication he gave in the creation of the book and for the precise editorial support.

Thank you very much to all Top-Creatives,

who regardless of numerous management duties, new business and other urgent matters, took the time for something important. I thank them for their generosity and openness, with which they made their knowledge available for the project "Pass Your Knowledge On to the Next Generation".

At the time of the interview, they worked in the following agencies.

Alencar, Mauro – Agenciaclick, Sao Paulo
Bastholm, Lars – Framfab, Copenhagen
Beyen, Karel – PMSvW/Y&R, Amsterdam
Bonomini, Enrico – DDB, Milan
Caballero, David – S,C,P,F, Barcelona
Carlson, Chuck – Duffy Design, Minneapolis
Carro, Javi – S,C,P,F, Barcelona
Cracknell, Andrew – APL, London
Denton, Mark – Blink, London
Drew Davis, Kevin – Wieden & Kennedy, New York
Duffy, Joe – Duffy Design, Minneapolis
Fernandez de Castro, Felix – S,C,P,F, Barcelona
Flatt, Kevin – Duffy Design, Minneapolis
Flintham, Richard – Fallon McElligott, Minneapolis
Frandsen, Rasmus – Framfab, Copenhagen
Freuler, Matthias – AEBI Strebl, Zurich
Gallardo, Juan – Thirsty Eye, New York
Garcia, Xavi – Casadevall Pedreno, Barcelona
Garfinkel, Lee – Lowe & Partners, New York
Goodby, Jeff – GS&P, San Francisco
Grabowski, Marek – The Hub, London
Gulbranson, Johan – Gulbranson Commercials, Oslo
Hegarty, John – Bartle Bogle Hegarty, London
Hoffman, Susan – Wieden & Kennedy, Portland

Hunt, John – Hunt Lascaris, Johannesburg

Isherwood, Bob – Saatchi & Saatchi, New York

Kitchen, Rob – CDP, London

Levy, David – Thirsty Eye, New York

Linne, Dave – MCLB, Chicago

Mackall, Bob – Freelance, New York

Macrone, Michael – Freelance, Dallas

Marabelli, Gianfranco – DDB, Milan

Mariucci, Jack – Freelance, New York

Matthews, Jon – Wieden & Kennedy, Amsterdam

Moore, Bob – Wieden & Kennedy, Portland

Moore, Jon – MCLB, Chicago

Nassy, Sean – Razorfish, New York

Packard, Wells – Icon-Nicholson, New York

Patti, Michael – BBDO, New York

Pereira, P.J. – Agenciaclick, Sao Paulo

Pogliani, Milka – McCann Erickson, Milan

Ponce, Hernan – VegaOlmosPonce, Buenos Aires

Raye, Katie – Wieden & Kennedy, Amsterdam

Reis, Abel – Agenciaclick, Sao Paulo

Roda, Ramon – Casadevall Pedreno, Barcelona

Sanchez, Angel – Casadevall Pedreno, Barcelona

Sann, Ted – BBDO, New York

Sandau, Mark – Fallon, Minneapolis

Sato, Mayumi – Icon – Nicholson, New York

Schaeffer, Lode – Schaeffer Wunsch Has, Amsterdam

Scher, Gilbert – Scher Lafarge, Paris

Schmidt, Barbara – Elephant Seven, Hamburg

Schneider, Don – BBDO, New York

Scholz, Anette – Scholz & Volkmer, Wiesbaden

Seidler, Peter – Razorfish, New York

Segarra, Toni – S,C,P,F, Barcelona

Serpa, Marcello – Almap – BBDO, Sao Paulo

Silverstein, Rich – GS&P, San Francisco

Simpson, Loz – CDP, London

Simpson, Steve – GS&P, San Francisco

Siqueira, Marcelo – Agenciaclick, Sao Paulo

Spencer, Paul – Y&R, Manhattan, New York

Stamp, Gerard – Leo Burnett, London

Taylor, Alexandra – Saatchi & Saatchi, London

Vega Olmos, Fernando – VegaOlmosPonce, Buenos Aires

Vince, Christian – DDB, Paris

Veelo, Edwin – Agenciaclick, Sao Paulo

Volkmer, Michael – Scholz & Volkmer, Wiesbaden

Voser, Erik – AEBI Strebl, Zurich

Waterfall, Simon – Deepgroup, London

Weinheim, Donna – BBDO, New York

Wells, Mike – Bartle Bogle Hegarty, London

Westre, Susan – Ogilvy & Mather, Paris

Wieden, Dan – Wieden & Kennedy, Portland

Worthington, Nick – AMV, London

Wünsch, Erik – Schaeffer Wunsch Has, Amsterdam

Zürcher, Hans Jörg – Advico Y&R, Zurich

If you are not, or only rarely quoted in this book, you will find the contents of your statements similarly formulated by one of the other Top-Creatives.

I. INTRODUCTION

Catch the Big Idea

The only reason I went into advertising was because of the ideas. They were also the reason I left advertising. There simply weren't enough of them.

Many Creatives shoot their ideas from the hip like a cowboy. That's cool. But most of them don't hit the target. That's not so cool. Shouldn't a professional only shoot once? What could be done to improve on that? Aim for the bull's-eye?

In advertising I saw many ideas come and die. They didn't die because somebody wanted them to, it just happened more or less accidentally.

Today, I know that it is not a coincidence when an idea dies – more a logical sequence. Because the briefing is wrong, because the client doesn't want any ideas, because one cannot describe the idea clearly; because we didn't fight for it in the presentation or because ...?

But there are positive influential factors as well. How else could a small few Top-Creatives win the Lions again and again every year in Cannes? This cannot just be a coincidence. Are there perhaps Creatives, who know more and aim better than the others?

In order to get behind this I quit my job as Creative Director to analyse, together with students at the Universität der Künste in Berlin, the winners from 9 international Creative Award Shows over the period of the past 7 years: Lions from Cannes, Pencils from D&AD in London, the One Show in New York and many others. Awards and over 7000 award winners were entered into the databank. Those with the most precious awards must certainly be brilliant Creatives!

Between 1996 and 2001, under the motto: "Pass Your Knowledge On to the Next Generation" I conducted interviews from this analysis with 77 Top-Creatives under the 100 best, worldwide. I questioned them on their most excellent works and on the process that these works were based on. I questioned them on strategies, client briefings, the work culture, the creative brief, the benefit of their communication, how they came up with their best ideas, how they evaluated and presented their ideas and which thought and work patterns they use in each individual working phase in order to arrive at exceptionally successful ideas. The result is shown very clearly by over 200 case studies conducted by IdeaManagement:

Great Ideas are no coincidence. They are the result of a great and fascinating process.

Not everybody is aware of this, but this process can be far more easily influenced than is generally assumed. Top-Creatives have rules for this that are described in this book.

A fisherman should be fishing in waters that contain fish. This is also a rule. A conscious one, an unconscious one? This is a rule that simply increases the probability of Catching a Fish. And for those who want to catch fish this is a good rule.

This book has been written for those who want to Catch Big Fish. It gives all communication professionals the possibility to examine their own personal "rules" and to increase their effectiveness in the Creative Process.

With many tips and just as many questions I would like to invite you to apply the strategies of the Top-Creatives, as a Creative, Account Manager and Strategic Planner, as a Junior and Managing Director, as a Marketing or Communication Professional on the client and agency side.

With every tip in this book you will be in a position to inspire and change the creative system in which you are working. Similar to pulling the corners of a tablecloth, you will be able to influence and improve the other areas of your company, or the work being done there, from every angle. And that is exactly what this book was written for. It is a workbook for those who want to have better ideas more easily and even faster.

Maybe one or the other section will remind you of what you have always known, and somehow forgot: that you yourself are an idea, that came into the world.

I wish you a really Big Catch in every possible manner.

Catch the Big Idea!

For whom this Book has been Written

Ideas are the most important thing in almost every profession. This book deals with the communication idea. The idea in advertising that fascinates people. It's about the ability to establish a target oriented suspense between people and products, which differentiates very good communication and is, above all, effective.

This book has been written for those who would do (almost) anything in order to bring a really Great Idea into the world. For those, whose demands on the idea are so high, that they always work longer on it than anyone else in order to overcome their own dissatisfaction.

It has been written for those who want to learn from Top-Creatives with whom they could probably never work together with. But also for those who believe that the development of ideas should have something playful about it, despite or maybe just because of clear rules and processes.

It has been written for those who know that they can work better and faster than they currently do, or the guidelines in the team or company allow them to work. Also, for all those who suppose that Great Ideas are not merely a question of pure luck and those who want to make use of coincidence to inspire themselves for even better ideas.

The objective of this book therefore lies in the description of best practices and work processes, with which international Top-Creatives achieve creative top performance more or less regularly. In order to show the spirit and self-conception of these Top-Creatives, quotes from interviews will be given to you verbatim. In order to be of most help to you in your day-to-day work, this book does not use any images other than those that come up in your head when reading it. You will not be looking at great work done by other people so you can concentrate completely on your own ideas – your own creative process. To make it as easy as possible, this book is structured according to clear work phases. It is a workbook and it will work for you and your ideas, if you make use of it.

As a junior or senior in an advertising agency or on the client side, it will help you to have more and better ideas in a far shorter time period. It is particularly helpful for you as a Copywriter, Art

Director, Creative Director, Project Manager, Account Director, Strategic Planner, Managing Director, Advertising Director or Communication Decider.

With every tip and the associated question you will be able to influence the energy and idea flow in your work process decisively, for your company, your team and simply for yourself. You can also achieve additional practical skills within the "Catch the Big Idea Workshop" in which the strategies presented there are trained in hands-on and practice-related exercises. Further information can be found at the end of this book and in the internet at www.catchthebigidea.com.

I would like to ask all female readers for their understanding that I have only chosen one gender form in some places to make reading easier.

»Shall we say, two per cent are great, shall we say one per cent are great, I think it's probably one. And there is a few per cent that are really good. Then there is a broad sphere of average, and then there is rubbish.«

Loz Simpson

II. Management Principles of Great Ideas

The Idea as the Highest Form of Energy

Have you ever asked yourself what an idea is before it occurs to you? And are you prepared to look at an idea, and see it from a different perspective?

Edwin Veelo: »*You feel connected with energy, you feel you are part of an energy, you are filled with energy and you feel like you can solve any problem. The moment lasts very short of course, but at that moment you feel very, very energized.*«

The symbols for the idea, like lightening and a light bulb, and also the subjective perception at the moment the idea comes to you, offer a new definition of the idea:

The idea is the highest form of energy.

John Hegarty: »*Great Ideas have an energy of their own and it's almost like creating life. It becomes bigger, broader, wider and it reaches out and affects things it touches. That's when you know you've got a Great Idea.*«

With what principles can such energy be directed or even be generated? Can you perceive the entry of this energy in your body, direct it through a complex production process, protect it and manifest it lastingly in its best form? For this purpose, you can associate the feeling when an idea happens with a very specific body reaction. By the way, it's a reaction that happens not only in your head, but also in your entire body. *Anette Scholz:* »*It is a general feeling of well being, but mainly in the stomach.*« *Matthias Freuler:* »*When my feet begin to tingle then I know it is a good idea.*« *What happens to YOU when you come up with a really Great Idea?*

1. *Do you feel the excitement in your tummy, the energy, that Wow feeling?*
2. *Do you have goose pimples all over or is your heart full of happiness?*
3. *Do you see the light or things clearly, how they fit together?*
4. *Do you feel a rush in your ears or can you hear when things go click?*
5. *Or can you smell a good idea from afar?*

You have to be completely aware about this – also when you are reading this book – because an idea travels with the speed of light. Within a nanosecond it pops in and triggers energy all through your body. Are your individual production processes ready for ideas in the speed of light? Can you keep and manage such a quick impulse?

»When everything is moving at light speed, this is it, I am there.«
Sean Nassy

Top-Creatives can generally keep and manage this energy better than others. But they are not satisfied with just having an idea. They see every idea as an investment that must produce returns to their clients, and that also carries hidden risks that need to be managed. For Top-Creatives an idea must function. It must sell something; work hard for the company, the brand, and the product. But how do you get an idea to work hard, if it appears in a nanosecond and disappears at the same speed? And how is it supposed to work if we think about an idea showing up is pure coincidence?

The Value of Great Ideas

Top-Creatives don't get their energy from thinking about award shows and creative prizes, but from the knowledge that they are an extremely useful service provider for their clients and their brands. They develop ideas as a multiplication factor for the advertising budget of their clients and achieve a return on investment, which is not nearly as much a matter of coincidence as generally assumed: *P.J. Pereira: »The principle that makes me start is never how to be creative. It is always I have to be effective, I have to talk to real people, I have to say things that people will believe, I have to touch them deeply. I never try to be creative, that is not the point. I am working on a business, I have to do something that brings results to my clients and that's what makes me alive.«*

A worldwide long-term study by the advertising agency Leo Burnett has been questioning responsible Marketing Managers for over 10 years, who have won awards for their communication campaigns. The result: over 85 per cent of the award winning work are also extremely successful in the market and 65 per cent of these prove this with hard facts or awards for their effectiveness.[1]

Consequently, generating great communication ideas means more than just pure creativity. It is much more about steering the attention of a target group according to the brand, the company and the product. The increasing flood of information does not make this any easier: *»The American Advertising Association says that of the 5,000 branded communications we are exposed to each day, we notice less than 2 per cent, and less than 0.1 per cent have any perceptual impact at all.«* [2]

At a time when attention is a rare commodity, a successful communication idea has a very high economic value.

Accordingly, successful brands are a result of great communication ideas. This makes it very clear why the client has to play a very responsible role in the Value Creation Chain. Case studies examined by IdeaManagement display this for adidas, Audi, Avis, Barilla, BMW, Coca-Cola, Disney, Hallmark, Harpers Bazaar, Heinz, HBO, Honda, IBM, Kodak, Levi's, Little Cesar's, McDonald's,

Mercedes-Benz, Michelin, Microsoft, Miller, Nike, Pepsi, Polaroid, Porsche, Samsonite, Silk Cut, Stella Artois, VW, Wrangler and several other very successful brands.

The general assumption that merely 50 per cent of the advertising budget is invested successfully does not hold true for these brands. Their value today generates more than 50 per cent of the value of the company, at BMW and several others even up to 80 per cent.[3]

Great Communication Ideas work hard. They create a huge added-value for the company. Not from coincidence but as a result of a consequently managed added-value.

---

[1] Does Award-Winning Advertising Sell (1994 - 2002), Leo Burnett, Chicago, August 2002; [2] GDI_Impuls 4.01, p. 17, Gottlieb Duttweiler Institut, Rüschlikon, Switzerland; [3] Marketingjournal 1-2/2004, p. 34, Enterprise Research Pricewaterhouse Coopers, Frankfurt, and Prof. Sattler, Universität Hamburg.

The Added-Value Power of a Nanosecond

For many, finding ideas is mystical and secret. But if you believe that ideas are merely coincidence, you must also automatically believe that the repeated success of Top-Creatives is coincidence as well.

>*The muse of ideas exist, but they have to find you working.*«
Xavi Garcias

You certainly know the expression: creativity consists of 99 per cent transpiration and 1 per cent inspiration. So the time before and after the idea shows up becomes the most important working phase. It not only determines 99 per cent of the work process but 100 per cent of time and costs, which play an increasingly important role in the creative business. It is transpiration, that forms the basis of a creative job, the actual value adding in form of a great communication idea however, happens in fractions of a nanosecond.

What makes the creative work so hard then? Do we not have a clear idea of what a Creative Process is? Are we doing things that are not necessary or even meaningless? Are we working very hard but in the wrong place? Anyone who manages ideas should be able to steer their energy professionally and hold on to it adequately. Because everywhere where energy is generated it can also be lost. Or is this not possible at all?

>*You can't lose an idea.*«
Javi Carro

When you lose an idea, you only lose the form of its manifestation. Perhaps a headline, a visual or an image. You lose one of maybe millions of possible images, but not the idea. If ideas are energy, then the laws of energy should also be applicable for the energy of ideas: >*Energy does not get lost it only changes its form.*«

According to this, the energy of an idea can exist in several different forms. Even its material density changes during its creation from the initial quick thought through to the finished and produced communication idea. When managing this density it is important to manage an idea in each working phase in a suitable and economic way. Otherwise, briefings will be too loose without describing a specific problem, or storyboards for presentations will be too final in their conception, sometimes with suggestions as to the camera angle, which should be determined by a good director at the appropriate time.

Both the too superficial and the too specific management of an idea therefore block the creative flow and make working with ideas so hard. But only an idea/energy that is managed through the Creative Process with the correct density will be able to flow and release the correct impulses. *Juan Gallardo:* »*It is a certain feeling, a certain connection of things where you know the flow is correct, you know, that's right, you just know it.*«

The building up and management of this energy from the initial job briefing up to the manifestation of a Great Idea is therefore not simply coincidental, but is subject to 99 per cent clear rules and principles, as in every other profession. Top-Creatives it is a quality controlled production process.

»*I believe that rule 1 is there are no rules.*
Rule 2 is there may be exceptions to rule 1.«
Loz Simpson

III. THE 12 SUCCESS FACTORS FOR GREAT IDEAS

The Most Important Added-Value Factors in Top-Creative Processes

In constantly successful creative companies, clearly defined high performance processes are at work that control the quality of the Great Idea.

The principles on which this quality control is based affect all working stages of the Creative Process. With these principles Top-Creatives set up optimal framework conditions, from the work culture, up to producing the idea with professional production partners long before the idea shows up.

For the development of the idea, each department provides its best contribution to produce a specific part of the creative product. If in doing so, a department in the beginning of the Creative Process only gives an input of 80 per cent, the follow-up department must build on these 80 per cent. Regardless, of which product is being produced the missing 20 per cent can never be reclaimed and compensated. If then the next following department also only gives an input with a quality of 80 per cent, the total amount to a quality has at this point already decreased to only 64 per cent. With these inter-dependencies each section of the Creative Process relies on the performance of the department before them. Concretely:

- ☆ Account Managers rely on the information given by the Client,
- ☆ Creatives rely on the information provided by the Account Managers,
- ☆ those presenting to the Client rely on the information given by the Creatives etc.

Accordingly, the application of Best Practices by each department optimises the quality of one's own work; in particular, it optimises the input for the next department and as a result, influences the desired end product, the Great Idea, in a positive way. But mostly this happens:

Garbage in – Garbage out.

The influencing factors that have an effect on an idea are obvious. An incorrect or uninspiring client briefing quickly leads to incorrect or less inspiring ideas. Fascinating and inspiring product information on the other hand, promotes fascinating and inspiring communication ideas. Input determines output; this applies to every phase of the Creative Work Process. From the initial contact with the client in new business, up to the finished communication idea.

What are the decisive added-value factors that allow Top-Creatives to repeatedly produce brilliant creative performance? How can you yourself influence the energy of an idea positively for your team or for your company? How can you hold the idea, manage it and turn it into a satisfying and effective creative end product?

The following 12 key factors will for the first time provide a comprehensive insight into the fascinating creative production chain of Top-Creatives from all over the world, and what they have in common. They will show you the specific work phases with which you can improve your own Creative Process. These work phases include individually

- ☆ the **idea-focussed company** vision that gives the Great Idea priority over other company goals, allowing a Creative Work Culture to develop,
- ☆ the **creative responsible and challenging creative client** that encourages Great Ideas and is not just open to them,
- ☆ the **fascinating client brief with an assignment** that defines the client's core problem in such a way that an inspiring and exciting perspective is given to the task,
- ☆ the **surprising and inspiring information** that provides deeper insights into the product, target group, competition and brand so the idea connects with real life,
- ☆ the **true and convincing strategy** that gives the idea direction and by which it can later be judged whether the idea is right on strategy and whether it functions,
- ☆ the **inspiring Creative Brief** with a single-minded proposition that both excites and focuses the team,
- ☆ the **playful, relaxed way to find an idea** that leads to surprisingly simple solutions that "show up" both in and especially outside normal work environment,
- ☆ the **professional description of the idea** that provides a clear impression of the idea, and differentiates between strategy, higher concept, core idea and execution,

☆ the **extremely tough evaluation of the idea** that is brutally honest, to exclusively judge the power and effectiveness of the idea,

☆ the **convincing idea presentation** that places the idea in the centre, and where only work is shown that you are honestly enthusiastic about,

☆ the **process oriented idea protection** that, with the belief in the Great Idea places the creative product in the centre of all business handling,

☆ the **sensitive and enthusiastic production of the idea** with new challenging partners who bring with their professionalism the idea up to an even higher level.

In the following chapters you will receive important tips with which you can

☆ increase the creative performance of your own team or company,

☆ specifically direct an existing work relationship towards Great Ideas and

☆ generate more and better ideas in the shortest possible time without losing energy along the way.

If brilliant ideas come about through hard work, you will learn from Top-Creatives how to design the Creative Process much easier for yourself and for your team in every work phase.

»I don't work, I play.«
Marcello Serpa

How to Create a Company that Works for Big Ideas:

The Culture

produces

An inspiring Company vision focuses the energy of all employees on one target.
That way the company itself becomes an idea that inspires. Such a vision strengthens all parts
of the Creative Production Chain and sets clear strategic priorities. This clear focus that
acts as a magnifying glass, sparks off passion and spirit. It creates a Creative Culture
that will stimulate Great Ideas showing up on a permanent basis.

the Work

Dan Wieden

An Inspiring Vision always Focuses on the Great Idea

Creative high performance companies give the Great Idea highest priority when they solve their client's tasks. That's what makes Top-Creative Agencies so magnetic and attractive. The necessary power arises from their inspiring company vision, which affects everyone who feels connected with the company, especially clients and employees. It is this priority of ideas that gives a creative company a clear direction that all the people involved can follow and be inspired by. This becomes even more important the bigger and more complex the company is.

Clear priorities allow employees to take risks and to try out new things as long as it serves the clearly defined target and is on strategy with the company's vision.

Dan Wieden: »We have three priorities. The highest priority is the work, the second highest priority is the client/agency relationship, and the third priority is yourself. As long as everybody is focused on the work, the client, your senior management, everybody involved, that seems to be the healthiest thing.«

Clear priorities also help in judging ideas and selecting new employees and clients. They produce a creative work atmosphere that has a positive effect on the development of a creative culture.

For Top-Creatives the Big Idea has the highest value in the company.

The more consistent the vision is stated and lived by management, the easier and clearer a company culture becomes manifested. This culture boosts the self-confidence of employees and encourages building up principles that support a system that repeatedly develops Great Ideas. In Top-Creative systems, from the first client briefing, up to the finished production, conscious and unconscious rules define what is important for the idea and what is not.

Dan Wieden: »When you start worrying about the client/agency relationship, it politicises the work. If you start worrying about yourself, that this is my idea, this my ego, this is my opinion, then you end up with some little star system and you can't see the work for the egos. You need to

get all that stuff out, and just be able to look at something. Is that good, is this working? Is it worth doing, or can I do better? You need to be honest about that. That's the fundamental tenet of the agency, and having fun.«

For that reason Top-Creative Agencies can be seen as energy centres because their procedures are focused on principles that build up energy for ideas very quickly; they manage and pass this energy on to their clients and employees.

Chuck Carlson: »Stay focused on the work and the magic can happen.«

While Top-Creative Agencies primarily concentrate on their work, there are agencies that are less creatively successful because of the lack of an inspiring vision, alternative goals and no clear direction of the company idea. The consequences are internal cycles in which the energy is used up for their own issues, e.g., politics and other mostly ineffective processes, instead of transporting it along to the client and their brands.

If for example the company profit is the main focus of the company vision, the idea, as the highest priority, takes a step back into the second row. It becomes just another important issue together with market position, growth, reduction of costs, maximizing profits, increasing shareholder value, increasing profits per head etc, and quickly looses priority. The real task of the company i.e., the generation of Great Ideas for clients gets pushed into the background. *Paul Spencer: »The reason there's a 95 per cent kill rate of ideas at some of the big agencies is because they find something else to do instead of the good work.«*

Today, only a few agency networks still really place the idea in the pole position. In order to examine just how attracting your company vision is and to check out your company culture, you should ask yourself the following questions:

☆ Have you got far more requests from clients asking for your creative services, than you can deal with?

☆ Did most of your demanding clients put the project in your hands without you having to do a pitch?

☆ Is most of the creative work in markets most relevant to you currently from your company?

☆ Do you have on-going job applications from employees who are also willing to work in your company, even for a lower salary?

☆ Does keeping to your company principles also cost you money or clients, so you can be sure that these principles are really being lived?

If you can answer these questions with "yes", then you can be sure that your company vision and the resulting culture works effectively. If not, change and improve your company vision. The following tips and questions will help you inspire your company or your team in a targeted way. They will support you in how to define, live, implement, expand, circulate and improve your vision.

Give the Great Idea the Highest Priority

In every Top-Creative system it is not about caring about personal relationships, or sensitivity, but again and again, it's about the very best work; with no compromises. *Ted Sann:* »**Absolute, absolute and total emphasis on the work. It sounds impersonal but it's not, because what happens in a lot of places is politics. You can be the greatest guy in the world, you can be everybody's best friend but if you come up with a shitty campaign you're going to be out the door! It's only going to be judged by what's on the page, or what you've come up with and what the idea is. People find that stimulating and exciting.**«

Under these circumstances, there is only little room for politics and other conflicts. The value of the idea becomes the all-determining benchmark. And good campaigns still remain the best reputation for every agency. They attract both good clients and talented employees.

*There is always the temptation of taking the easy route
and doing what the client wants and collecting money.*

Joe Duffy

Joe Duffy: »*There is always the temptation of taking the easy route and doing what the client wants and collecting money. If you do allow yourself to go that route inevitably you will be doing work that you are not proud of and that has a snowball effect. Creative integrity is incredibly important. It has a tremendous effect on our reputation.*«

**Which routines do you have to break
in order to put the idea first?**

Communicate Major Principles Bindingly and in Writing

Many companies lose a lot of power because they do not write their visions bindingly. They keep a little back door open so that they can always change principles and react more flexibly if needed. It is through this back door that you lose power, credibility and energy. A vision, like every Great Idea, is something you are totally convinced of. This long-term conviction allows an inspiring company culture to grow.

John Hegarty: »*Culture is what keeps the company going. It's what allows it to grow, and not lose what it's about. Culture comes out of beliefs of what you are doing and how you are doing them. Our culture (at BBH) is written down and we have our ten guiding principles.*«

A great company vision describes the idea of a bigger and brighter future. And top management has to make sure that the principles that allow this inspiring vision to become true are lived. That way it can develop a creative culture that is truly stable and stimulating for Great Ideas.

Katie Raye: »Wieden & Kennedy is a pretty unique place. It is not run by the accounts guys to execute some kind of business model. It is all about the creative and Dan Wieden leads the place. It is all about doing what inspires you, so that is a really great environment to be in.«

*Which of your company principles inspires
employees to Great Ideas?*

Encourage Flat Hierarchies

Flat hierarchies promote and allow for quick changes with which creative companies can overcome existing limits. They reduce internal regulations to the minimum, make meetings and resolutions more effective and more efficient, and allow for quick and unconventional decisions. This gives you more time for ideas.

John Hunt: »I don't think ideas travel through a bureaucracy very well. We are very flat-structured and there are no real fancy titles in the agencies. We are all on the same level. We are probably about 250 people and we also get rid of a lot of the politics.«

*Could a person in your company from the bookkeeping department
have a Great Idea that would be produced?*

Create a Culture by Placing the Highest Demands on the Idea

Top-Creative agencies challenge their employees to make the highest demands on their work. Because very good work can inspire several others, in particular the tough evaluation of the idea is essential. *Bob Moore: »In prior agencies the work was judged in 'Gosh, does this meet the brief'. Here it is judged in 'Gosh, is this something that I haven't seen before? Or is this something that feels really fresh?' The emphasis is more on something that is new and different. More risky I think.«*

In such a challenging work culture the employees can invest their entire energy for the good of the company. This makes the company culture the most valuable production factor. *Dan Wieden: »At the end of the day the culture produces the work a lot more than the people. It's the attitude, the sense of freedom, the sense of expectation and the level of performance that is acceptable. That's what creates the work.«*

Most people don't realize how strong a creative culture and the respective processes work, until they go to work in other places, and find themselves no longer achieving their usual creative performance. And even those with less talent, often achieve much better performances when working within an inspiring company culture, because they have the opportunity to work with superb tools and other challenging people.

With which project are you going to start excellent work today?

Keep the Creative Company Culture Alive

A culture that intends to bring new things to life must be alive itself; otherwise it cannot adapt, develop and grow. It would be caught in its own status quo.

John Hegarty: »Ultimately, the culture of a company is constantly changing, constantly evolving. A culture is not a fixed thing, it moves and develops as time goes on. For me, culture is a fundamental aspect of an agency's lifeblood. I've got to create a culture which allows people to do the best they possibly can, there are guidelines, there are rules, there are principles, but they are not encased in stone.«

Only if the people working within the culture experience it as being alive, a mutual exchange of knowledge and support will happen. Then the system inspires the employees and employees inspire the system. *Bob Moore:* »*Wieden & Kennedy is a funny place, you learn more from the creative people here than you ever could anywhere else, I'm convinced.«*

> *How can you personally ensure that an inspiring company culture can be experienced?*

Make Your Creative Management a Physical Experience

Top-Creatives live their high demands as an example, and this helps others to experience them. This also includes also "public criticism" of work that was just not good enough. *Kevin Drew Davis:* »*The expectations are really, really high, Dan Wieden sees all the work, he still sees every single thing that goes out of here. If you put out a crappy ad you're going to hear about it, people are going to send you an email, it's like dear I saw your spot, horrible!«*

Kevin Drew Davis

In order to be physically close to their team, some Top-Creatives work without a personal office. *Marcello Serpa:* » *I don't have a room, no room of my own or the like, I sit with everybody together, around 25 Creatives, with assistants, right smack in the middle. I don't try to have a room of my own or any of these hierarchical notions.«*

For active confrontation with the idea other Top-Creatives have installed a special form of meetings that let them experience their Creative Leadership. *Hernan Ponce: »We show all the work and discuss why the account guys don't sell that or what we can do. It was an interesting way of changing the whole agency.«*

Do you regularly reflect on your work and take the consequences from the result?

As Creative Director, do not be in Competition with Your Team

Top-Creatives make sure that their employees have the best conditions for the job. If you, as Creative Director, are also involved in the daily working process and develop ideas yourself, you will quickly have a problem being objective when it comes to evaluating these ideas. *Bob Mackall: »We had a hard and fast rule that we would not compete with anyone working for us, that definitely would be unfair. I think it's difficult when you have pride of authorship to be totally objective.«*

Those who want to be equally good both as a Creative and as a Creative Director often do not fulfil either task brilliantly. Top-Creatives create an inspiring and caring atmosphere in which all Creatives can stand their ground, not against each other, but against own high creative standards. *Steve Simpson: »One thing that Jeff Goodby and Rich Silverstein have been really remarkable at, is they really care about their creative people and helping them realise what their best idea is. Helping them understand their own idea and making it as good as it can be. They don't look at a problem and say, 'How would I solve it?', they want to see how you're going to try and solve it.«*

How do you help your employees to permanently improve on their best ideas?

Create an Exciting Atmosphere through Exciting Jobs

The inspiration power of jobs influences the agency culture much more than most people are aware of. Courageous clients who approve challenging and brilliant ideas are therefore extremely important for an energizing creative culture. *John Hegarty:* »**The energy comes out of the excitement of being here. Being able to do it. It's fantastic being given these opportunities.**«

Xavi Garcias

Top management at the agency must initiate this enthusiasm and attract exciting jobs that excite employees to come up with Great Ideas. This positive feedback cycle is the fastest way to establish an exciting atmosphere.

A creative culture originates from a work atmosphere that allows you to make your own work as strong as possible and lead it to the highest energy level.

What exciting job could stimulate your work atmosphere to be even more inspiring?

Pitch against Your own Work before Others Start to do it

Because Top-Creative agencies are never satisfied with their own creative product they do prefer to pitch against their own existing work. Sometimes using a new Creative Director. *Andrew Cracknell* on Carling Black Label: »*I was partly employed at WCRS to sort out that specific campaign. Over the next 3 or 4 years we actually turned that campaign around and it became quite good, very good actually. The brief went up to the whole creative department, I actually had about 40 scripts and you have to make the correct choice.«*

One main reason for the use of outside help to change existing work, is sometimes the internal doubts in the agency whether a creative campaign is possible with an existing client at all. *Andrew Cracknell: »Up until then the creative department themselves had been very sceptical about the campaign. They didn't think it was based on a particularly good piece of thinking, so they weren't that optimistic.«*

It is a courageous decision to optimise the creative work with the help of outside employees. But again: It is much easier to do this when the Great Idea has top priority.

Which campaign from your company or team would you like to pitch against immediately?

Make Sure You Give Inspiring Work Energy when Criticising

If an employee is caught in mediocre work, coaching the employee can easily become a personal and professional challenge. Particularly when criticising their work, you have to keep the employee's positive work energy. *Jeff Goodby: »You have to keep their energy up during the process, and I think that's where a really good Creative Director comes into play, in a situation where the idea isn't particularly good yet and you have to help them go back and start over. You're basically*

Make the process fun for you
David Levy
and the people you work with.

49

saying to them, everything you've done so far is not good, but you have to find a way to say that so that it doesn't sound like that.«

As the name says, the Creative Director sets the creative direction. To do this he should define the direction for his team and manage the process so that employees can develop new and improved ideas out of their own strength. Top-Creatives therefore ensure an inspiring work process and input for their teams long before the idea shows up. *Bob Moore: »We see all the briefs before we let them go to a creative person. We look to see if it is interesting. If not, then Mr and Mrs account person has to go back and take another crack at it. Because it's either (a) not clear enough, (b) too long and confusing, or (c) the challenge isn't as provocative as it could be.«*

What would inspire you, your team or your employees more effectively?

Test the Idea Internally as Early as Possible

In many teams ideas are developed almost secretly. However, the earlier the work is internally made public to everyone, the sooner everyone can get a crack at it and improve it. Some Top-Creatives hang the idea up publicly in the early stages – in order to increase the challenge and to shape the idea into the best form possible. *Mark Denton: »Anyone in the creative department of the office could make any comment they liked on it. And any team who thought they could do a better ad could try to beat the concept that was on the wall. That was our system trying to get the best out of everything.«* This work process was used for every job regardless of which client it was and what brief it was. *Mark Denton: »Everyone was ruthlessly ambitious and that's why we hired people who wanted to get on and who were talented as well. If you are a good creative you know if someone has got a better idea, and if you are honest with yourself you don't argue.«*

Any team who thought they could do a better ad
could try to beat the concept that was on the wall.

Mark Denton

So, each individual could bring up the internal standard to the highest possible level. As long as the creative product is put in first place, a healthy competition arises, instead of envy and jealousy. *Richard Flintham: »When they beat you with an idea you learned from that, nobody was really fighting anybody afterwards. It was great.«*

What measures can you take to initiate
a competition for better ideas?

Give Juniors Important Jobs

Though experienced senior Creatives have a lot of knowledge, this can also block them. Young talents can bring a completely new perspective into existing situations, often due to a lack of experience. New ideas can arise from this ability to interpret things without any baggage. *Milka Pogliani: »They have got fresh eyes on everything. They don't get into the cliché or the stereotype, they don't use formulas.«*

John Hunt describes just how important the unburdened impressions of young teams are: *»We often find our best ideas come from our most junior people. We never enter junior competitions. We have some 18/19 years olds who have won Gold Lions at Cannes. It's often where the freshest ideas come from, the very young people who haven't been tainted by advertising, haven't been told these are the rules.«*

In your company how often do junior teams work with
responsibly on big important projects?

Promote the Creative Chance instead of the Higher Salary

In Top-Creative agencies the best creative idea wins. This is the highest prize for a creative team and the reward is independent of title and salary. *Mark Denton:* »*They could steal any brief they wanted. If a junior copywriter came in and said they have a better idea, than we would do theirs. We encouraged a sense of ruthlessness. Anyone who wants to make a mark for themselves has just got to try that extra bit harder.*«

Mark Denton describes how attractive a mutually challenging standard is: »*No one joined our place and got a rise, wage rises were slow, purely based on performance. In a lot of places you win one big award and you could get your salary doubled. If someone won an award I gave them five hundred quid. That wasn't a rise.*«

What creative chances can you offer instead of a salary increase?

Trust Your Best Employees Utterly and Completely

In many agencies teams are set against each other in order to strive for a better creative product. What is decisive here is that this working against each other is held up by a common vision and not from doubts on the quality of the employees. Many Top-Creative teams prefer to do without this competition.

Steve Simpson: »*We tend not to have different teams compete against one another because I think the best way is to hire good people and give them a responsibility to figure it out on their own.*« With this trust, the commitment and the entire energy is used for the client, the job and the idea. And it encourages "Problem-Ownership". Splitting responsibility always leads to the splitting of energy and motivation.

Susan Westre: »I find that's demoralising for teams because they like to have ownership, like I own the problem and I have to solve it.«

The best way is to hire good people

Steve Simpson

and give them a responsibility.

Trust provides energy and as a result it creates the best conditions for professional work on the idea. *Kevin Flatt:* »**This company supports myself and the people here 100%. There is so much belief in the people that work here that I have never had a situation where someone has not pushed to make sure that he is doing the best that he can do.**«

How do you show your employees that you trust them completely?

Look for a Partner Who Inspires You

Top-Creative teams could also be called strong "mini-companies" because a productive work culture can also originate with only two partners. In a strong team the partners give each other mutual inspiration. *Don Schneider:* »**Michael (Patti) and I click together creatively better than anyone I have ever worked with. I just hear a phrase or a word, and I'll just start running, he can say something, and boom, I'll wake up.**«

This kind of mutual inspiration has lead to many foundations of new agencies. *Dan Wieden:* »**I didn't really take it all seriously until I met Kennedy and he showed me how to take one of the most dishonest professions in the world and really try and infuse it with something that had your own ethic about it, and do work that was challenging and interesting.**«

Dan Wieden

Inspiring partners awaken the best part in the other person and help them develop their true potential. They mutually push each other to a new, higher level. *Dan Wieden:* »**With Kennedy it took on a whole new level of meaning to me, a sense of crusade about it. Dave came from a group of people that were a sort of underground in advertising. They refused to do bad work, they refused to do what clients told them unless it was something they could be proud of. There was an ethic and a personal standard that was higher than the standard of the agency, and higher than the standard of the clients and that's what they had to answer to.**«

Does your partner awaken new creative characteristics in you, if not, why is he/she your partner?

Make the Highest Demands on Your Employees

One other effective way to inspire an agency culture is to acquire new brilliant employees. They have a direct influence on the atmosphere, and their advantage is that they don't know how the system worked in the past.

Jack Mariucci: »**Working around a lot of good people makes you better. You're more eager to do better work, if there're 3 or 4 great people in your office, the level just rises very quickly.**«

With great people a far higher standard is put on the work. *Alexandra Taylor:* »**It comes from the energy of being inspired from seeing something, getting excited by it and being around people** *who are doing good work. You feel slightly more under pressure because you know you have to produce great work.«*

Alexandra Taylor

To create an inspiring atmosphere Top-Creatives place the same high demands when evaluating Juniors, as they place on their day to day work. Every new employee defines the creative environment in which the Great Idea originates. So you should make sure that you get the best and most creative employees. *Ted Sann: »I think we have to make it tougher to get in here.«*

What would increase your demands on new employees considerably?

☆

How to Make your Client a Great Creative Director:

Not only was the client open to great work

Would you hire your client as Creative Director? No? Then you have a problem.
He already is your Creative Director. Nothing that he does not release,
authorise and approve will appear as an idea. Every client should be aware of this huge
responsibility towards the Creative Product. And any good Creative Director is
not only open to good ideas – he demands them emphatically.

he **demanded** it

Steve Simpson

The Client has to Support Creative Top Performance

The client is the first and last decision maker in the Creative Process. He describes his problem in the beginning and judges the results at the end. And sometimes the client demands a better creation than the agency has presented. In this situation the client defines a higher standard on the creative product than the agency, and so takes over the role of the Creative Director.

For this reason, Top-Creative agencies agree with the client at the beginning of the project, about what criteria the creative work will be evaluated on later. The client takes over the role of a "Pre-Creative" and helps to prepare the Great Idea. *Susan Westre:* »*It doesn't matter how good the creative person is. If the client will not work with you, you're not going to get anything good out. If you go to award shows to Cannes, and you see the stuff, half the credit goes to the client. A good creative is nothing without a good client.*«

The main requirement for such partnership is mutual respect. You can only mutually achieve added-value, if you mutually value each other.

Recognising the others worth increases the mutual trust for courageous ideas.

Mutual trust gives every partnership energy. Mistrust takes this energy away. And trust is so important in order to carry the risk of new ideas together. Giving trust and energy to each other also has economic advantages. It reduces unnecessary control and helps to discover new playing fields together. Trust speeds up work processes and reduces transaction costs.

That's why "Pure Income-Clients" can be expensive for an agency. While they bring in income they often hinder the outcome, i.e. Great Ideas. That's why Top-Creative agencies, before they accept any new business, make sure that energy flows easily and safely when dealing with the Client. So sometimes Top-Creatives even make clear demands on what person has to fill key positions on the client side.

Susan Hoffman: »*They offered us some other brands that we didn't want. Other people there were overseeing the brand that we didn't want. So we basically handcrafted who we wanted to work with and what part of the brand we thought we would be the most successful on. That was the most unusual way to get a piece of business. But I think the chemistry was right and that's why we asked for certain people to work on it.*«

Clients who follow agency employees to new agencies without knowing what the result of the creative work is going to be in the future, show how stable this chemistry can be. It is based on trust and mutual appreciation. Though from a good client, Top-Creatives demand far more.

Bob Mackall: »*He first of all demands great work. Second he needs no test to recognize great work. Third, he has the money to run it and to buy work, even if it happens to be on the expensive and elaborate side. Fourth, he has the courage to run it. You find this usually when the client owns the company. You find it with entrepreneurs, often in smaller companies. You sometimes find it when the company is about to go bankrupt and they have no choice but to try to do something different and dramatic.*«

Often clients and agencies are only ready to risk everything when they have nothing more to lose. The more there is at stake the more courageous they have to be. This is particularly true for big brands, where with increasing success, the fear of risk taking increases at the same time. The bigger the market share, the more courageous the decisions have to be, and the appropriate positions should be filled with courageous people on the client side.

Hansjörg Zürcher: »*Companies that start to panic because of a bad reader's letter will never have unusual advertising. Fear is an significant factor and a significant idea killer on all levels of management.*«

Fear can only be overcome if both the client and the agency continually place the highest demands on the creative idea in an atmosphere of mutual trust.

In order to check whether your client-agency relationship is suitable for Great Ideas, you could ask yourself:

- ☆ Are you really proud of your clients or of your agency?
- ☆ Do you manage to bring Great Ideas into the world together on a regular basis?
- ☆ Do you feel that your partner values and inspires you in every way?
- ☆ Do you have the courage to try out new and risky things together?
- ☆ Can you rely on your business relationship 100 per cent?

If you can answer these questions with "yes", then your client-agency relationship offers you the best conditions for creative top performance. If not however, you should ask yourself why you should work on jobs with a partner that you don't trust and don't value? Surely not just for economic reasons? Perhaps the following tips and questions will inspire you. From the agency and/or client perspective they are always focused on the Great Idea.

See Your Client as the Creative Director

Work, which is not released by the client will never appear, for this reason it is important that the client and agency criteria are in agreement and satisfy the highest standards of a very good Creative Director. Proof that this is possible in admirable relationships is shown in the example of Volkswagen. *Gianfranco Marabelli: »One of the most important creatives in Europe was a product manager. Another one is Creative Director in England, he's a supervisor for Volkswagen and he was marketing director before too. Normally the account people wanted to work for the clients. At VW it's opposite.«*

Good clients also have good ideas. *Enrico Bonomini: »The actual creative spark here came from the client. In fact, the client was watching a crash test with the dummies and thought that was a good idea for a commercial. In this case, it was easy to develop the idea, we didn't have to change it very much.«*

Clients who have no desire to work for the agencies as Creative Director should ask themselves what qualifies them to evaluate creative ideas.

Which client could be hired as Creative Director, which one could you develop into one and which one would you have to fire?

Acquire Creative Business instead of New Business

New business is a very effective possibility to change an agency and/or to establish new creative client-agency relationships. With every new business the rules of the relationship can be redefined. But be very choosy with which partners you become involved with, as whoever you connect yourself with, also connects themselves to you.

Joe Duffy: »Half of the time we will say 'No' to potential clients that come to us. We ask very difficult questions to our prospective clients so that we know that we can pave the way to do the best possible work, work that we can be proud of. It's so important that it is a collaborative process and the clients want us to do great work as opposed to just getting something done.«

Half of the time we will say 'No' to
potential clients that come to us.

Joe Duffy

Not every new client is a client who wants unusual ideas. That's why Top-Creatives check right at the beginning of a new client relationship whether both partners place the same high standards on the creative work. *Richard Flintham: »If you have the right sort of conversation at the beginning of the process, everybody leaves that particular meeting with an idea of what they should be doing and what they should be expecting, or how they can make this better, rather than being shocked in three weeks as a client, 'Oh God, that's not what we thought'.«*

According to what criteria do you define mutual standards long before the presentation of the first idea?

Expand the Specific Creative Playing Field for every Client

In existing client-agency relationships, Top-Creatives have a clear image of what suits the client and what suits the brand, and just how far they can lead the client beyond their creative limits. *Dave Linne: »If you're trying to sell something that is not within their personality, it's going to die. You can always push the envelope a little bit. Go to the edge to make them do something that they have never done before. Make them a little bit nervous, but you can't cross that line. There are definite boundaries you have to work with, there's a playing field, and you have to play within that playing field.«*

Go to the edge to make them do something that they have never done before.

Dave Linne

The consistent direction towards such playing fields then leads to significantly quicker results. *Mark Denton: »We won awards on something like 75 per cent of the ads that came out of the agency, so almost every client we worked on won some kind of award somewhere, and over a five or six year period we won over 400 awards.«*

Clients who know that over 80% of the creative campaigns that have received awards are extraordinarily successful in the market too, also appreciate the value of such awards from a monetary point of view. They don't just make their budget work hard but they also make the idea work hard.

How do you recognize when you have led your client to a new creative limit, and how can you expand this creative playing field?

Say what You are Thinking Openly and Honestly, even if it Means Arguing

Arguments and rows are productive when you are arguing about a better idea. In particular, for big and economically important clients an open and critical word is of great importance. After all with their size they bind a lot of power, personnel and energy.

Simon Waterfall: »*I learned in many ways that you can be very, very honest with people, even huge, huge clients.*«

Those of us who believe that the confrontation with ideas is a harmonious process will prefer to water them down instead of fighting for them against common conventions. *Angel Sanchez:* »***The essential element for fighting is: not giving up and having the balls. The sense of courage is something necessary to be able to provoke, so people don't feel indifferent.***«

I learned in many ways that you can be very, very honest with people, even huge, huge clients.

Simon Waterfall

By standing your ground, you make it easier for yourself and others to work with you. And you will become quicker, because you are expressing yourself clearly and distinctly. *Marcello Serpa:* »*We always say what we are thinking. You are wrong, that is lousy, that is shit. And the client sometimes listens to us and sometimes he doesn't and then we have a huge argument. Usually if the client respects the agency it runs without any big hitches, but sometime you have to be pretty hard.*«

If you want to create unusual things you cannot always have an ordinary opinion. Get used to the feeling of thinking differently and live with the fact that sometimes you won't even be liked for that.

To whom would you now honestly say that you don't really like the idea that was sold?

As a Client, Become Enthusiastic about the Product

The passion of the client for a product is absolutely necessary because it reveals new fascinating information, which can be used to spark off new exciting communication ideas. For example the Automatic-Campaign for the VW Passat in which thrown away left shoes were shown, was sparked off by discussions with the client.

It was probably the most money we have ever spent. Six trips to the factory to talk to the designers from where the idea came from.

Richard Flintham

Richard Flintham: »It was probably the most money we have ever spent. Six trips to the factory to talk to the designers from where the idea came from. They are just obsessed with their cars.«

"Obsessed" means that that the client also has to be obsessed with the Great Idea for his products and services. Very often however, for top decision makers on the client side communication is only a small part of his entire work field. *Bob Moore: »You need to have a client who is excited and passionate about what they are doing. If they are just marking time until their retirement, you know that they are not really going to want to do some fun, good stuff. You've got to want to do it.«*

How can you as a client pass on your obsession with your product to the agency?

As a Client, Put your Agency under Creative Pressure instead of Time Pressure

Many clients make demands on their agencies in the wrong areas. They are not clear enough in their demands for a new, unusual, fresh solution, they rather demand a solution in time. In the worst case scenario, the agency will prefer to deliver on time rather than ask for more time to work out a really brilliant idea.

Steve Simpson: »Not only was the client open to great work, he demanded it.«

Clients must not just tolerate or expect creative top performance, they should demand it. Right from the beginning of the process they should make their high standards clear because he has a right to unusual ideas, which will multiply the power of his budget. However, work on a Great Idea is active work – also for the client. And the client should be more than prepared to carry the consequences. That means, more work and discussions right up to the risk associated with really new ideas.

Does your agency know that you demand really Big and Courageous Ideas?

Give Your Agency Time for Top Ideas

You can't program Great Ideas. They happen, and the probability that they will happen grows with the amount of time invested. Sufficient time also creates the possibility to throw away good solutions and to look for better ones.

Edwin Veelo

John Hegarty: »*It's like making a great sauce. It just takes time. I have never found a way of short-circulating that. You always say, why can't I make this process quicker?*«

More time makes better ideas because their manifestation is more mature. *Edwin Veelo: »It's like a good wine, it needs time, peace and a rest to get better.*«

When it comes to finding ideas however, some Top-Creatives can see time pressure as a positive boost. *Lars Bastholm: »Everybody likes to have plenty of time, but I think the real effort comes when you can start to feel the pressure.*« The most important thing is that every Creative can define the dose of the time pressure, as he needs it. Because, depending on the preferred work

process, deadlines can either make you more productive or block you when time becomes
too tight.

*Do you give your business partner sufficient time
to give brilliant results?*

As a Client, only Buy Ideas that You Like

Many clients simply buy what the agencies present to them. If, however, two or three mediocre
ideas are presented, they don't even have to be extravagantly tested because you already know that
they are not good. You always have a right to Great Ideas. Insist on this and demand the best of
all possible solutions.

Steve Simpson: »*Ultimately clients should not run stuff that they don't understand or that
they don't feel comfortable with. It is no victory to sell something to the client if they don't want
to buy it. Or if they are reluctant to buy it. You want them to be whole-heartedly behind it.
Because ultimately my name does not appear at the end of the commercial or at the bottom of
the printed ad. It is their name that does and it has to represent their company. It has to be true
to their voice.*«

*Ultimately clients should not run stuff that they don't
understand or that they don't feel comfortable with.*

Steve Simpson

If you are not 100 per cent convinced of the idea, you should not buy the idea. It is better to start
off afresh with a new idea where everything is in place and exciting, than to try to improve a

mediocre idea. If an agency does not set high standards of creative work in order to achieve exactly such standards, then the client certainly has the right to set the standards himself. However, you as the client, should also provide the right conditions with time, trust, information, openness and other factors described in this book. Only then can you expect Creative Top Performance from the agency.

What does your agency need in order to deliver
even better ideas to you?

Demand Courageous Decisions from Employees, instead of Correct Ones

In order to release an unusual idea that provokes and polarizes, you have to have courage. It is practically impossible to generate attention from something really new and risky and at the same time not to assume that at least a few people will be bothered by the idea. In the end, that is exactly the aim of a Great Idea, to shake people up and to say something new to them.

Mediocre advertising is liked by everybody,
Xavi Garcias
because it offends nobody.

Matthias Freuler: »Of course you have to expect that we will annoy 100 or 200 people but on the other hand we will say something to 1000 people that convinces them that this product is really somewhat cheeky.« Unusual ideas tend to polarize people, to also get attention.

Xavi Garcias: »Mediocre advertising is liked by everybody, because it offends nobody. Water is liked by everybody, it's very healthy, but it has no colour, no taste. Coca-Cola, however, is not liked by everybody. But when somebody likes it, he likes it a lot more than water.«

How do you encourage your employees to really unusual and risky new work?

Encourage Client Contact to Creative Employees

Top-Creative agencies transmit creative energy to clients first hand instead of using the Account Manager as the "energy buffer" towards the client. They allow Creatives to present their work themselves so the spark can jump over directly.

Bob Moore: »The first thing we do is if an idea is approved by the Creative Director, the creative people go and sell it to the client, they go and present. And so they are enabling their client to participate on the passion and excitement they have for what they did. We make it the creative person's responsibility to get a client fired up about an idea, not the account people, that's not fun.«

Unless you feel supported by them
Michael Macrone
you are going to withhold your best work.

But not only the client profits from this direct impression. Top-Creatives search for closeness to the clients so that they can get information and inspiration first hand and also have greater creative freedom. *Michael Macrone: »I feel most uncreative when I have no communication with the client, either they don't understand me, or I don't understand them. The best situation for me is if I feel there is a spirit of experimentation.«*

This feeling of trustworthy closeness promotes personal commitment towards the client and as a result, really brilliant work. *Michael Macrone:* **»Unless you feel supported by them you are going to withhold your best work.«**

How can you make sure that creative energy can jump over more directly and more personally?

Establish a Creative Challenging Relationship – or Dissolve it

The basic requirements to avoid mediocrity, are trust, honesty and openness. In order to find out just what makes the client tick and whether he is suited to the agency, Top-Creatives enter into a very close relationship with the client from the very beginning.

If you feel like you are wasting your time, you shouldn't be there. Not only are you not doing any work but you're dedicating spirit and energy.

David Caballero

Lode Schaeffer: **»We always insist on talking to the client and getting to know the client from the very beginning. You have to know the heartbeat of the client, of the company, to know whether it fits in that tradition, and the way they see their market and how they treat their audience.«**
His partner, *Erik Wünsch,* expands: **»I think close contact to your client and his problems is essential for getting the best ideas. If you look your client in the eyes and keep talking with him**

about the product that you're going to make advertising for, then you really hear his doubts in the market, his worries in the market and you hear a lot about the market itself.«

This closeness gives you a far better perception of the client. *Matthias Freuler:* »*The most important thing is that you really know everything about the product and that you were present at the briefing yourself. That you played around a bit with the client to find out how far you can go with him, how can I get him enthusiastic about something?*«

The intense tuning with the client also holds consequences for new business and the development of ideas. *Erik Wünsch:* »*We never start doing a pitch with creative work because we believe that making a creative work is a process you have to go through together with your client.*« If the relationship to the client is not okay then Top-Creatives quickly act accordingly. They say "No" to a client that does not have the courage and the passion for Great Ideas.

David Caballero: »*If you feel like you are wasting your time, you shouldn't be there. Not only are you not doing any work but you're dedicating spirit and energy.*«

How can you make your client-agency relationship more challenging and more honest?

How to Transform a Great Problem into a Great Idea:

The most enjoyable
part of the job is

Top-Creatives get their energy from the assignment. They know that an idea
only has value when it solves the problem. That's why they rewrite the client brief
until it describes a great problem, to then solve it with a Great Idea. In the end also
a problem is just an idea. However, it's an energetically highly condensed idea.
That's why we say, some problems are difficult to solve.

cracking
the problem

Loz Simpson

The Client Brief as an Exciting Challenge

Some tasks are more fun than others. Why is that? It's a question of our perspective. Top-Creatives change the perspective of the problem to be solved, for so long until it becomes fun to solve it. So they re-formulate it and discuss it for so long with the client until a position is found out of which the Client Brief becomes inspiring and exciting. And a good briefing excites both the client and the agency. Because:

>*There is a gem in every single problem.*<
Juan Gallardo

"Input determines output" takes on a whole new meaning here because only a really exciting challenge will excite and inspire the team. However, simply renaming the problem into a so-called "challenge" is not sufficient. On the contrary, it requires "a very good idea of the problem".

Bob Isherwood: >If you can work out what the problem is, then the solutions seem to come quite easily and naturally. It's defining the problem that's difficult, and you can't do that unless you've got a lot of facts.<

50 per cent of problem solving is defining the problem. Finding the problem is therefore also as much a Creative Process as finding the idea. Much too often, we still talk about solutions for problems that nobody really has. Looking at the problem until it is understood and makes sense ensures that "light comes into the darkness" at an early stage, and an initial idea of a relevant and exciting task can show up. This relevance and excitement give an assignment energy and fascination.

If this is not given, the task will block instead of inspire. The result is then a briefing that is unclear, which will lead to repeated, endless loops of discussions, but not to a clear starting position for the development of strategy and ideas. So, often the actual idea of the Client Brief doesn't become clear until the client presentation, when then a Re-Briefing is given by the client. This is highly ineffective and frustrating for everybody involved. For this reason:

Put the job in the right position, before you start
to put yourself on the job.

Otherwise, you yourself may quickly become part of the problem. This happens easier than you think, because as a "professional problem solver" you're applying to solve other people's problems. In order to do this, you have to put yourself in their place. But if you do not keep an objective position and begin to "understand the client only too well", you may easily get caught up in the problem yourself.

For this reason, free-lance consultants or agencies have a big advantage: They are just circulating outside of the problem and/or the company, looking at the job with the eyes of the market.

Gilbert Scher: »*We usually present the client a new way of presenting a problem, and when it's okay we start. It's another kind of perspective.*«

It's called problem solving, because you have to dissolve the problem from yourself and the client. This demands giving up a normal position in order to discover something new. Let's face it, an idea does not just come from nothing. It has to be sparked off by hard and really exciting facts.

If you want to know if your Client Brief is already exciting, you can ask yourself:

☆ Do you find the assignment challenging and could you already describe new aspects of it that fascinate you and others?
☆ Do you have access to information that would give you a far better or new understanding of the problem and provide you with new insights?
☆ Can you feel the great creative potential that lies in wait for you and your team?
☆ Are you honestly inspired by the new relevant aspects that this new task is showing you?
☆ Are you eager to solve this problem in a completely new and surprising manner?

If you have answered these questions with "yes", then you have an inspiring briefing and will easily be able to solve the problem. If not however, you can ask yourself why you accepted the job in its present form at all? The job is already boring you. In any case you need a new perspective of the problem. Make use of the following tips and questions in order to re-define your briefing.

Describe the Main Problem in one Sentence

Just as many strong ideas have weaker ideas close to them, real problems also have side-problems close to them that steer our attention away. That's why it is important to discover the main problem so you know what angle to go from. Solving the biggest problem also releases the most energy.

Hernan Ponce: »**I try to get all the information that I can, try to write it in two or three sentences, try to detect what the problem is.**«

This means you should be able to describe a big problem in one or two sentences just like you describe a Big Idea. By concentrating on the "Big Problem" – similar to the Big Idea – you ensure that in the continued process you will be working with a "really juicy problem" which will release enough energy to form a Great Idea and a solution that works hard in the market.

Loz Simpson: »**You have to crack the main problem.**«

How do you describe the main problem to someone on the telephone, in one sentence?

Re-form the Problem, until it Inspires You

Normally, we are influenced by many other thoughts when we are defining the problem. This is not always worthwhile. *Karel Beyen:* »**Usually somebody comes with, this should be in there**

and this should be in there. I try to get rid of all that crap and all the directions people give you. I want them to make the problem as clear and naked as possible.«

I have to formulate the problem
in the way I feel there are ideas for it.

Karel Beyen

Bob Moore: *»Figure out the problem until it's exciting, and when it's exciting you have the excitement to do the idea.«* Restructuring the job will make sure that the energy from the problem can flow into the next stage of the process.

*How can you talk about the job
in a simpler and more exciting way?*

Make the Problem Simple and Single-Minded

In every phase of the Creative Process it is important to simplify things and reduce them. This also holds true for the problem. *Karel Beyen: »When somebody explains something to me then I cut it down to something really simple. First I try to make it a really simple problem.«*

We can much more easily concentrate on a single problem, and not double or multiple problems, to then come up with a clear solution faster. *Karel Beyen: »When somebody has written down the problem, the answer is already there, I only have to find it. Usually I really only work ten minutes, that's what I like, if it's a simple problem.«*

Such a simple focused thought is also called "single-minded". A single-minded problem is the preliminary stage of a "single-minded proposition" later in the Creative Brief and is of course

Karel Beyen

extremely valuable. *Juan Gallardo: »There is a gem in every single problem. I always go back to that because I really truly believe that, that there is a unique answer, a message to be from whomever. We all have our stories to tell and only if we listen will we understand.«*

How can you reduce the job to an even more simplified problem?

Reduce the Problem to a Challenging Question

Too many briefings are boringly written and are not challenging for Creatives. They do not inspire. They give answers instead of asking questions.

Dan Wieden: »The best assignments are trying to figure out what is the question we want to ask, not what is the answer to the question. So a good assignment is always a question. The best strategy is a well-defined question.«

Dan Wieden

Such a question fulfils several important criteria. *Dan Wieden:* **»You don't automatically know the answer to it and it comes out of the heart of the issue, the strategic issue you are trying to deal with. There has to be an unresolved issue there. What is the thing, we can't quite solve?«**

A good question places the problem in a new perspective and withdraws energy from it. If this happens in an inspiring way, this energy can be used to develop new ideas. Everything we question, we resolve and de-manifest up to a certain point. This is also true for problems.

What inspiring question can you gain from your problem?

Let yourself be Briefed on the Problem, not on the Solution

Often, already at the briefing, the client tells you how the problem is to be solved. This means that the framework for unusual solutions is too narrow. *Hernan Ponce:* **»When a client says I want this, this and this, okay – but what do you need from me?«** As a result, the definition of the problem is already a creative task. *Susan Westre:* **»We get awfully trapped into what do we think our client wants us to say which might not be the right thing. If they knew, then maybe they wouldn't need us.«**

Only when freedom of thought exists to discover completely new ways and forms, also in a precisely expressed briefing, can we develop unusual ideas. *Angel Sanchez:* **»I always ask for a margin of liberty that goes right up to the end so that we can always change things.«**

With this agreed liberty the Creative Process remains flexible and open in all phases for unexpected perspectives and an even better implementation of the idea.

What do you think the actual problem is, and from which point of view can you define it even better?

Use Market Research for Problem Definition

Market research can be, together with Strategic Planning, an instrument with which the early phase of the Creative Process can be improved. *John Hunt: »**Research is good at telling you about the past, but it's not so good about dictating the future.***«

Top-Creatives use market research in particular to qualify and secure their information input. In many Top-Creative agencies Strategic Planning assumes this function from the perspective of the target group. *Steve Simpson: »**I'm not adverse at all to using market research and focus groups to find out what the markets think about these clients. I find that kind of consumer research much more useful and interesting at a really early stage of the process than at a later stage when they pretend to evaluate work.***«

Research is good at telling you about the past,
but it's not so good about dictating the future.

John Hunt

Market research at the beginning of the process helps to build up new views and information, so you get a clearer and more focused impression of the actual job. It also helps in the development of relevant key messages.

What reliable market data support your problem definition?

Write a Briefing that Really Excites You

Very often the client doesn't know exactly what information the agency needs. That's why it is important that all the information is put on the table that's suitable to describe the problem, and

to become really excited about it. For the outside observer this information usually leads to completely new perspectives very quickly. Look for the problem first, not the solution.

Rob Kitchen: »Firstly I need to know that the people who are briefing me have done their homework, and know exactly what it is that needs to be done. If you're not inspired by the nature of the problem that they are giving you, then you can't work.«

Rob Kitchen

If the client himself is not fascinated by the job why should the agency/team be fascinated? Just because they get money for it? This is not a basis for a creative connection that could lead to a strong idea. It also means that the worth the client gives the agency is probably low. An agency or a Creative Department is not a dump for jobs that nobody wants to process, but rather a creative high performance laboratory that needs the best possible input from its suppliers.

Would you like to solve the problem yourself right away, and if not, what is missing that excites you to do it?

Write a Precise Briefing for a Precise Evaluation of the Idea

Being precise in the description of an assignment means reducing things to the minimum. But wherever you leave something out you have to take responsibility for what was left out. "Brief" means "short" and here as well the creative principle of reduction generates excitement. This makes writing a briefing a challenging creative task.

David Levy: »***Working within limitations is always easier.***«

A good analysis of the problem helps to bring the briefing to the point, and it is a universal misconception that a wide, unspecific briefing is better because it does not limit the Creatives. *Edwin Veelo:* »***I need limitations to create, I need to feel the walls to be able to kick through those walls. If everything is possible then where do I go. I haven't lost ideas through limitations, I have got ideas through limitations.***«

Since creativity always needs to be sparked off by something, Top-Creatives prefer clear facts and focus to ignite them. This focus works like a magnifying glass. *Felix de Castro:* »***I work better with a limited brief than with a very wide one. If I had to choose between one of the two, I'd rather have a narrow brief than a wider one.***«

Working within limitations is always easier.

David Levy

In particular, unusual ideas need a clear rational backup for their defence. An imprecise briefing is therefore a bad basis for the evaluation as to whether the solution corresponds to the job. Such a briefing can already destroy a Great Idea before it was even developed.

Is your assignment specific enough to measure the quality of idea on it later?

How to Gain an Insight, that Makes a Difference:

Interrogate

the product

Ideas do not appear from nowhere. They spark off on conscious and subconscious information. The more information you have available, the more material you have to develop an idea. The truer and more surprising this information is, the more powerful the idea will be later. An effective idea will always be "anchored" in fundamental information, preferably about the product, because that is what you are trying to sell.

until it confesses

Rob Kitchen

Information, the Material Ideas Come from

Top-Creatives spark off their ideas on true and surprising information. So they research the product in every way possible. They carry out a kind of "Creative Market Research". To anchor their
idea in reality, in the product and in the target group. They know that with better information
they will arrive at better ideas quicker.

*Gilbert Scher: »We are looking for the truth, you can't create or invent the truth, you have to find
it. Often we go to the company to look at the product. We need the material premiere, it's in the
company, it's in the product, and after we can model it.«*

The partial obviousness of such information, which others could also recognize and use, can really
put pressure on you. *Michael Patti: »I get nervous that someone else is going to do something similar because it seems so obvious and so simple.«*

Everyone who has ever received very interesting information in a client briefing that immediately
triggered off an interesting idea will know how fast great information triggers Great Ideas.

Surprising insights quickly lead to surprising ideas.

This is also true the other way round: without surprising information it will be difficult to arrive
at new and interesting ideas. Because information is always available in a certain form, in order to
work with it one should not initially interpret this information. Neither positively nor negatively.
Information is a material which will later be transformed into a new meaning for communication
purposes.

*Wells Packard: »Look at everything, even if it is something you have seen before you have to
look at it again.«* Only those who can perceive new and surprising aspects in normal things will be
able to have new and surprising ideas about them.

Top-Creatives could therefore also be called "alchemists" because they have the ability to transform information material from one form to another.

In the Creative Process the client assumes the role of the information supplier. The better the information is supplied, the simpler and faster the processing of an idea will be.

But all too often, the contact people on the client side change, and the product and marketing experts only have superficial information available, instead of in-depth knowledge, background and connections. In order to gain unique information Top-Creatives go out searching themselves. Similar to a very good chef de cuisine who chooses ingredients at the market himself.

Lars Bastholm: »I need background information, I need research, I need focus groups, I need as much information about the client and the target group and about the product as I can possibly get.« With this information Top-Creatives make up their minds and build up their own valuable theories. *Alexandra Taylor: »Little nuggets of thoughts can make you a beautiful, simple and very powerful commercial.*« Long before the idea is found they search like gold diggers for insights, knowledge and understanding within the problem and in the job, They know:

>*»Every product has one great campaign in it.*«
> Mike Wells

Top-Creatives look for exciting information to trigger new thoughts and they know the risk of missing, bad or false information. In order to solve a task, it is therefore absolutely necessary to make yourself completely familiar with the problem and/or the product, so that you can gain facts that you can newly interpret later.

The more fundamental the truth that is hidden within the information is, the bigger the energy is that can be released into the idea, and of course, the more people can be reached by it. This is particularly important for ideas that should function worldwide. The more international an idea has to work, the more universal this truth must be.

In order to determine whether you really have new information available when you communicate, you could ask yourself:

- ☆ Do you already have truly surprising information on the product, service, the company or the problem environment?
- ☆ Do you know exactly what makes the target group tick, what really interests them, or where they have a problem?
- ☆ Have you already been able to gain new insights and knowledge that could spontaneously inspire you to several good ideas?
- ☆ Do you know what hidden characteristic(s) make your product unique in the market and therefore differentiates it?
- ☆ Do you know what language your brand speaks, what it needs, what suits it and what not?

If you can answer these questions with "yes", then, for your later strategic work, you have enough information available with which you give relevant direction to an idea. If not however, how are you going to make something out of nothing? You need true and really great information as input for the truly Great Idea. The following tips and questions will give you additional inspiring information for your ideas.

Interrogate the Product until it Confesses

In many agencies the Creatives do not take the time to occupy themselves extensively with the product. This means that only superficial information is available, which the client has passed on to the agency with his briefing. Superficial information leads to superficial ideas. So also here, the principle – "input determines output" – is valid.

Top-Creatives go to the client themselves, they go to the production, talk to the individual departments and try to find the little stories behind ideas or hidden in the product.

*Rob Kitchen: »**Interrogate the product until it confesses.**«*

It is necessary to really interrogate, because the product knows something that it is not confessing to everybody, and this unique and in-depth information must be identified and/or processed first. *Rob Kitchen: »Keep at it until it brings up the one thing that is unique in the market. Where everybody is making very similar things, the consumer is confused, I am confused, so how am I able to tell the people, this is better than everybody else's? You have to give me reasons why. That side of the business is very scientific, logical and process-lead.«*

Keep at it until it brings up the one thing that is unique in the market.

Rob Kitchen

Often during the product examination or production, you discover individual characteristics that are extremely interesting and surprising, and probably only known to professionals or users. A client, Marketing Director or Product Manager that does not have this information available is forced to express himself loosely. It is not very unusual that the above-mentioned groups are not consciously aware of these interesting characteristics. In order to get specific information and ideas you are going to have to go search for them yourself.

Where can you find additional interesting information
on your product?

Get Excited about the Product

Belief in the product and the excitement about it will intensify the confrontation with the product, and make the search for new surprising information easier.

Bob Moore: »**You have to believe in the product, that's the main thing.**«

Every product has one great campaign in it.

Mike Wells

Doubt and underestimating the product on the other hand will withdraw energy and excitement. *Susan Hoffman:* »**I wouldn't be in this business if I just had to do advertising for advertising's sake. I truly believe in the brands I work on.**«

Only with openness, nosiness and excitement, is it possible to discover something new in a product or a brand that nobody else has discovered yet. This is the material that Great Ideas are made of. *Mike Wells:* »**Every product has one great campaign in it.**«

What makes your product so unusual and fascinating?

Look at the History of the Product and the Brand

Important information and a good "anchor" for unusual ideas can also be found in the history of the product or brand. Many brands are decades old, so the story of its origin in the founding years could contain important information. This is made clear by the work for Wrangler Jeans in London. *Nick Worthington:* »**We were in America, and we met a guy who was an ex rodeo-rider. He was telling us about all his stories. He had broken 27 ribs. He had broken pretty much all his**

body in the course of his rodeo career. We subsequently started working on Wrangler and found out that Wrangler's main heritage was with rodeo riders. That's what the jeans were originally designed for. We did some research on rodeo and met lots of young and old guys who were just like this. You have your storage tank of stuff in your brain, but quite often you need sort of triggers to get it going.«

Some information can also be found in personal records and collections of committed employees. *Nick Worthington: Most companies have got some kind of archive. Every company will have something like that and the thing to do is to get into that place and to have a good root around. That's fun. You will find out lots of stuff.«*

You need sort of triggers to get it going.

Nick Worthington

Also talk to the complaints department. They often have an even better access to various information sources. Remember, the employees in this department are busy trying to limit damage when customers are unsatisfied. For this reason they have to know more and be more competent than others.

Do you know the history of the product and where the internal company archive is?

Look in External Archives, Bookstores, Libraries ...

Gathering information outside of the company often brings incredible information to light that you can directly connect to ideas. You can find this information in internal or external archives,

databases or libraries and also in professional magazines, client journals, internal publications and sometimes also in the press department.

Bob Mackall: »You've to go to the public library or a bookstore and just browse through the category. I look for any information I can find on the category that maybe the product is in.«

New impulses arise from new input, new perspectives, new questions and also new areas, which have nothing to do with advertising. From art, technology, through contact with sculptors, musicians, journalists, doctors, lawyers, clerks, chefs etc., real people that do something completely different. *Jon Matthews: »Whenever I have spare time I go straight into the book stores, straight to the record stores and look and see what's there. I like fresh stuff, I like fresh data, it's not because you want to be the first to use this photographer, it's more a case of being influenced by from outside of advertising.«*

What other information from the environment of the product would surprise people?

Interview Long-Term Employees of the Company

People who have been working for the company for a long time can also give you important hints. For this reason, sometimes the doorman can be a better person for the Creative to talk to than the Marketing Director.

Nick Worthington: »Talking to people is one of the main things, because people always know much more than they think they know. When you go to a factory some of the people there will just know stories about the product, they will know a lot of its history, they will know all the little weird things that they have done in the past to make it better, or to make it work. So it's

useful talking to those kinds of people, and it's useful talking to the people that have worked for the company for a long time. They are not the kind of marketing directors that tend to change every year.«

Talking to people is one of the main things, because people always know much more than they think they know.

Nick Worthington

Experienced employees often have a lot of unofficial knowledge, of the company, the founder, the culture, taboos, written and non-written laws. You can compare the process of gathering information to searching for truffles, and you know how much they are worth. It is even possible, that the people who would have the most to say about the product and so could provide you with important information or stories, are no longer with the company, maybe they are retired. Ask for them in the personnel department and get in touch with them!

Which unofficial contact person has the most intimate knowledge of the product?

41 Attack the Product in Order to Discover its True Destiny

All to often we are satisfied with boring information and superficial explanations. It is worthwhile to go one step further. In this context, offensive attack and questioning the product or the service of the client, offers you a good chance to get more and better information. The counter-arguments will then provide you with important answers that you can use in communication. This will help you to get a clear idea of the advantages and strengths of the product.

Rob Kitchen: »*I immediately criticise the product as much as I can to the account people or the planners, or whoever it is who's giving you the brief, to basically say what it isn't. It's not good for this, it's not good for that. This is for me to understand what it is going to be about because all advertising only ever shows the good side.*«

If Account Managers or Product Managers are not capable of defending the product, it will already become clear at this phase of the Creative Process that one will have to think again about the job and the product.

I immediately criticise the product as much as I can.

Rob Kitchen

Milka Pogliani: »*It is not just to hurt them but just to tell the truth, and if you tell the truth you are never wrong.*«

Which hidden facts about your product has nobody ever discovered or communicated?

Look for a Personal Truth in the Product

Whatever people can perceive together offers a solid basis for new ideas. This is one of the reasons why all of the classics in advertising literature insist on the sentence: good advertising is true.

Nick Worthington

When you've got something that's coming from the heart, then it's much easier.

Discovering a deeper truth in your subject is one of the greatest challenges, and respectively, a chance for every Creative. Regardless of whether you are an Account Manager, Strategic Planner, Copywriter or Art Director. The power that is hidden in this truth is absolutely substantial.

Dan Wieden: »The most powerful things you do are trying to get at the truth of something. I think most good work is personal. It's hard. If you can't find something interesting to you, you have to start there. You have to have a personal relationship with that challenge you are faced with, and the truth you are dealing with is not some sort of universal truth, but it is the truth to you in that subject. The best work has that sensibility about it.«

You have to have a personal relationship with that challenge you are faced with.

Dan Wieden

That means Great Ideas are honest and should touch you personally. *Nick Worthington: »Bring some real sort of passion, or some real feelings, or some real motivation into it. Because if you're always trying to just manufacture stuff, just trying to invent things, it's very difficult, but when you've got something that's coming from the heart, then it's much easier.«*

The first person to discover such a truth can make use of it. That is the reward of the work. Many products have kept it hidden up to today. Their truths have simply not been discovered yet.

What surprising truths are there about your product?

Plan some Time for Orientation and Information Input

Top-Creatives schedule several days for orientation that is important for the gathering of information. These are even more valuable if the Marketing Department has only little know-how of the particularities of the product.

Mike Wells: »We're often sent on orientation days for looking at the production process, talking to as many people as we can, trying to find out something different about the product or something unusual which you can anchor the idea in.«

The length of time that needs to be scheduled can depend on the complexity or availability of the product and can be between one day and one week. Working without this specific information almost automatically leads to exchangeable ideas. This kind of conscious information input especially stimulates the incubation period in which the idea can mature.

Mike Wells: »The trick is you have to pump your mind full of as much information about the product as possible and then wait for something to pop out.«

Find out something different about the product
or something unusual which you can anchor the idea in.

Mike Wells

The orientation period must be calculated into the timing and costs. It is part of the work. And a part that is worthwhile. In the end it is better to have quality information at the beginning of the process, instead of having to correct the idea again and again at the end.

*Have you planned fixed orientation days
in your time and cost schedule?*

Examine the Product with the Eyes of the Target Group

Many ideas in advertising have absolutely nothing to do with real life. Partly, because they are too fantastic in order to be real, partly because they are too ad-like to be true. However, there are lots of exciting stories, which nobody has ever told. Top-Creatives look for these stories, and question lots of people on possible information so they can develop stories to.

A creative person needs to take their own ego out.

Steve Simpson

Nick Worthington: »Talk to as many people that know as much as possible about that area. Some of those people will be in the agency, and some of them won't be. Some of them will be people that run shops and people that sell the product out on the street and other people that use the product.« Very often we forget that an "un-likeable product" also has a reason for being and can also present an attractive solution to a problem for a certain group of people. That's why Top-Creatives always see the product or problem with the eyes of the target group.

Steve Simpson: »A creative person needs to take their own ego out of it and try to see what it is, what the product is, what its truth is in the world, what it means to people and then create a consistent voice for it. It shouldn't be part of your own style or part of an agency style.«

What stories do users, consumers or sales people tell about the product?

Start Your Own Market Research

In Market Research and in Strategic Planning there is the danger that information will be kept out or get lost. This means that important triggers for ideas are reduced because somebody else

researched the situation instead of you yourself. *Jack Mariucci:* »*Planners can very much pinpoint you and that's helpful in a lot of ways. In other ways, it can sometimes hinder you because if you're going down a very narrow path, the real idea might be out here to the left somewhere or to the right.*«

For this reason, many Top-Creatives get personally involved in the planning and in the extensive "examination" of the relationship between the product and the target group. *Kevin Drew Davis:* »*Someone said that the best creatives are the best planners. You have to watch people, you have to watch how people react.*«

What makes a cornflakes eater a Heavy User? You don't know, ask him. *Susan Hoffman:* »*Go and find somebody that's passionate about cornflakes, that loves them, interview people, find out. You know 'I think I work faster if I eat cornflakes, I don't know why', if that's the truth then go and find that person, go and find out some special memorable things about your product. Don't wait for people to come to you, go and do your own stuff.*«

When are you going to start your own creative "Market Research" to speak to the target group personally?

Look for Exciting Impulses and Impressions outside Advertising

Many Creatives are not always open to unusual impressions, although these offer especially important input for new ideas. *John Hegarty:* »*It goes back to having an open mind, letting influences*

You have got to keep an open mind because you don't know where it is going to come from.

John Hegarty

come in, hearing things which are interesting, keeping them in your mind, having them around you. You know they are all there, they are floating around. There is something also about things that are in the ether, things that are in the atmosphere. You have got to keep an open mind because you don't know where it is going to come from.«

If you look at it that way, the idea, and respectively the information to get transformed, is already around you. It is already in the atmosphere. *Juan Gallardo: »I believe ideas are everywhere. I believe anything can bring that gem, that pearl. There are triggers all over the place and usually that is just walking down the street, just looking in windows, just looking at people and to many other elements.«*

I believe ideas are everywhere. I believe anything can bring
Juan Gallardo
that gem, that pearl. There are triggers all over the place.

Most of us know the expression that someone is putting out his feelers. But just putting them out is not enough. We have to be switched on, so that the signals we receive can be processed. *Javi Carro: »This work is like being a sponge. You absorb things from everywhere and then at one point you squeeze. And the squeezing can be done either here, or at home, or on the weekend. So the result is you never know when it's going to come out.«*

What exciting information outside of advertising could have a connection to your job?

How to Give an Idea a Clear and Relevant Direction:

Truth

is the best strategy

Great Strategies are Great Ideas. They are a new interpretation of known, true information.
With strategy, true product information is transformed into relevant benefits and strong promises.
The strategy gives the idea a direction, the content and the What the communication should express.
A good strategy is both relevant and creative – this is what makes it so effective.

anybody ever had

John Hegarty

A True Strategy Delivers a Truly Good Solution

The communication strategy condenses all found information to the most relevant Creative Message. The energy of such a strategic idea should be apparent. It develops from the subjective feeling of coming a great deal closer to the solution and of having found a message that will solve the problem. As the strategy is the first half of the solution.

> »50 per cent or more is strategy. Good creativity is impossible without strategy.
> Strategy is creative, and creativity is form.«
> Xavi Garcias

In Top-Creative agencies the Strategic Planner is therefore closely connected to the Creatives. They sit and work in the Creative Department. This secures the idea and also helps to sell unusual solutions more easily. Also the title Creative Director says in the name, that the Creative Idea has a "Direction" and so can also be planned and directed.

Top-Creatives place a great amount of attention to this direction. So they talk to experts and consumers. In this way they can discover truths and insights within the context of the target groups and products, which inspire new messages. Allowing them to lay down the direction of the idea later. *John Hegarty:* »**Truth is the best strategy anybody ever had. First, it is the most powerful strategy you can have because it disarms people, and second, it is true, and you can't deny the truth.**«

In new business, several Top-Creatives just present whatever brilliant creative thought they think can solve the problem. And somebody who can explain a solution understandably, doesn't have to go right down into detail, in order to sell it. That is effective and cost saving. If such a strategy is missing, many Creatives develop their ideas on chance or they develop the strategy later on, instead of developing an idea that is already on strategy. One can hardly imagine more meaningless meetings, than ones where the ideas are being discussed or evaluated without any knowledge of the strategy and in absence of reliable criteria.

For Top-Creatives, differentiation between strategy and the idea is very important – for the development and evaluation of the idea.

>>*The deeper you dig into the strategy the wider the way to work creatively.*<<
Felix de Castro

A well-established and approved strategy has several positive effects on our subconscious creative potential. It ensures that your thoughts are clearly focussed on the job; and even a severely limited strategy allows for more effective, larger creative scope than no strategy at all, where everything is open.

In addition, if the strategy is missing, a subconscious part of us is simultaneously occupied with drafting a strategy in order to give the idea meaning and content, so as to justify it. This withdraws energy and attention, which you could use more effectively to develop new and even better ideas.

In order to check if your strategy is relevant and creative, ask yourself the following questions:

☆ Does your strategy connect true facts to a new inspiring view of the problem that is seen as the solution?
☆ Does your strategy have an outstanding idea that will excite the target group in a relevant manner?
☆ Is the idea of your strategy new, focussed, and does it also carry a certain risk because of its reduction?
☆ Can you honestly sell the strategy as an independent creative product and have it approved by those responsible.
☆ Does the strategy give a clear direction, so that it is also suitable for the evaluation of very unusual ideas?

If you can answer these questions with "yes", you have already developed a strategic basis, and in fact you have already solved the problem. All you are missing now is a good idea of how to communicate your solution in a new way. If not however, are you going to evaluate whether the idea is right later and on strategy without a strategy? The following tips will help you to transform your information into a new relevant strategy.

Start Your Own Creative Planning

"The whole world talks about Strategic Planning, in former times this was just called common sense", a Top-Creative mentioned recently. Another definition says: "Planning is creative thinking based on information". That's why Creatives should not delegate thinking to another department or person. *Richard Flintham: »I think we are very strategic in the way we think as creatives. We will probably get more satisfaction out of a strategy than we would out of an execution.«*

I actually think creative people are the best planners.

Bob Isherwood

The development of a strategy is creative work, as we are talking about the forming principle of reduction. It is the creative interpretation of the information gained that helps to come up with a really new idea from a simple strategy.

Bob Isherwood: »I actually think creative people are the best planners.«

Lee Garfinkel: »Even though we have a planning department, I make it everybody's responsibility to participate. I don't care where the idea comes from. I would rather everybody sit down and have brainstorming sessions on how do we position this car, how do we position this soda.«

One of the biggest advantages of Creative Planning is that it gathers valuable information from which the Creatives can draw their own conclusions. *Jeff Goodby:* »***Sometimes it's a really small thing about a product or the people that use it. Other times, it's the lack of information that makes you think clearly about it.***«

How can you express the solution to your task in the form of one logical, relevant message?

Talk to Experts about the Problem

Many people working in the Advertising and Marketing Departments do not have a real in-depth knowledge of the specific product or problem, usually because they have only been working for this company for a few years. That's why it can be worthwhile to look for strategic solutions in expert circles: internally within the company with professionals, service departments, research and development or, externally in universities with professors, specialists, scientists and other sources. You will seldom find inspiring facts in the office itself.

For the local police campaign, *Bob Isherwood* sent his team directly into the night: »***They spent a couple of nights in police cars and they came back with about 20 ads, and when they went to the client, they went with new information, and the client was going 'wow', this is incredible.***«

If you really want to understand your product, research it. That makes it easier to understand the relationship between the product and the target group and/or service and the public. It is the deeper understanding of these connections that leads you to new ideas and a relevant strategic message that already delivers 50 per cent of the solution.

Which specialists, congresses and trade fairs on your product or theme do you know about or visit?

Examine the Product Playfully

Playful behaviour with the product and its task helps to change your perspective of the product or of the problem of its target group, so that you can discover new aspects. This will help you to get new information and triggers for exciting strategy ideas and new promises.

The confrontation and the personal experience with the product are absolutely important for most of the Top-Creatives in order to get unique information. Even if they are only based on the well-known decimal point-error regarding the amount of iron in (frozen) spinach. *Angel Sanchez:* »*I picked it up and started playing with it a bit, it was so hard. It seemed rock hard. I thought this is more similar to a piece of something than food. And from that moment, I just basically thought it was a piece of iron. Iron that you can eat.*« This playful method of observation led to the idea that a magnet could attract a child that had eaten spinach.

You will also get relevant information through the history of the product, its characteristics, certain form, and possible uses, information that is written on the product or its packaging or how it is manufactured. It is really important to use this playful examination for products where you would not imagine this kind of information with a superficial look, products we would call homogenous.

Nick Worthington: »*On Levi's there are product points about the jeans. You can start working, on the aspect that famous people wear them, or what materials they are actually made from, or how long they last, or the first pair you ever bought. There are loads of angles that you could approach a problem from. Go to one, exhaust that and if you want to jump, then jump if you have a thought.*«

What three unusual features about your product
would really surprise people?

Look for Real Disadvantages

Disadvantages can also provide a unique, still relevant promise. This is because truth itself does not differentiate between "positive and negative". In this way you can get new ideas from what appears to be a problem. You just have to take the problem by the horns. If it is a unique problem it can inspire you to a unique strategy as displayed by a job for Wrangler.

Mark Denton: »The kids hated Wrangler, they are the jeans my Dad wears, terrible. I have never seen such a negative reaction. They had picked on that 'W' stitching as the manifestation of everything that was worth hating about Wrangler. So we had to make the 'W' sexy, something that all the kids wanted. We did that by saying, 'Be more than just a number', which said be an individual and which was based against the 501 Levi's.«

This example shows clearly that there is no such thing as negative information, but that you see its value in the interpretation. Information that is thought to be negative, if it is true, can give out positive energy and move you to new ideas.

What negative characteristic of your product can inspire you to a positive message?

Look for Benefits in the History

You can usually also find a strategy basis in the history of the product or brand. The advantage of this information source is that the conclusions arising from this are easy to sell to the company, because they are part of the company's or the brand's history. This is also displayed in the spot from Levi's "Launderette".

John Hegarty: »It was going back to the roots of the brand, when the brand was at its most interesting. It was at a time when rebellion occurred amongst teenagers, which was a mythical time in the 50's or maybe early 60's. It was with the likes of James Dean, Marlon Brando, people like that, who were, in a sense, the first 'teenage' stars who were rebellious, and they had the 501 as part of their rebelliousness.«

The confrontation with the history of the product often provides you with much true information that sparks off new ideas and interpretations for the future.

What relevant strategic message can you find out of the history of the product, the brand or the company?

Always Defend the Point of View of the Target Group

The most important thing in the life of a product is the consumer and/or user. His wishes have priority over the wishes of the client. *Xavi Garcias: »It's important to know how to find what the consumer really wants, this is what the creative has to think about. Because the manufacturer is only thinking about the money he is spending in the factory. The creative has to be with the consumer.«*

For this reason, Strategic Planners are also called the lawyers of the consumer. They become immersed in the life of a consumer, understand him with all his judgements, prejudices, fears and worries. Only then can you arrive at surprising statements.

Xavi Garcias

Milka Pogliani: »You have got the ideas when you are really digging into the story, the product story, the consumer story. The more you are in, the more you can get out of it.«

Defend your target group, in particular in front of your clients, marketing and all of the columns of figures with which consumer needs are usually explained. Use your common sense.

From what specific viewpoint of your target group could you develop a strong strategy?

Explore the True Emotions of Your Target Group

In order to solve the problems of a target group, Top-Creatives not only explore with their heads, but also with their hearts and feelings. This helps them to interpret existing relationships between products and people in a new way, and from a strategically relevant angle. *Ted Sann: »The consumer isn't an object, nor a subject in an experiment. The consumer is a person like you, and the business that we are in is making contact with consumers on behalf of our clients.«*

The art of mass communication is setting up a relationship with unknown people. This is also the reason why so much advertising is entertaining, and works with humour and feelings. Whatever people laugh about, whatever raises them up to their unique perceptions and experiences, is strong and true for them – not only as a target group but as a human being. *Ted Sann: »You really have to get through to them and break through on an emotional level, which we believe is the only way you sell anything to anybody. You have to find something in the essence of the brand, or something in the product that resonates very one-to-one with the consumer.«*

These perceptions are also called insights. They offer a surprising understanding of the motives that move people to do something, or not.

What insights do you have on the emotional behaviour and viewpoints of your target group?

Be Simple but do not Treat the Consumer as if He were Stupid

In order to formulate a simple and attractive strategy proposition, it helps if you put yourself in the place of the consumer. However, don't strain the target group with too much information. Remember, you only have an attention span of a few seconds to transport your strategic proposition, an attention span that you get with your idea.

If people can possibly misunderstand what you're saying, they will.

Rob Kitchen

Always have a positive attitude towards the people with whom you want to communicate, and keep your message simple. Do not imagine that the consumer is stupid. Who would want to put himself or herself in the place of a "stupid" person? *Javi Carro: »I never do advertisements thinking that the consumer is stupid, or is not going to understand this. I don't like to talk to people as if they were stupid. Don't treat people like idiots.«*

What would make your message even simpler and easier to understand?

Look for Something Special when Shopping for the Product

Great Ideas often give us a great perspective on human behaviour. By observing shopping behaviour you can also discover interesting relationships between the product and the target group that you can use for a strategy message.

At FNAC, for example, it was noticed that customers in the CD department often sing the title of the song, unfortunately, however, so badly that it is almost unrecognisable. The message: "A professional FNAC salesperson will recognize it anyway". *Christian Vince: »In this department store there is something incredible, the people who sell the records are terribly good. If you only know the sound of the record but you don't know the artist, or the title of the record, then you sing it and they find it. They're incredible, so we play with that.«*

For Top-Creatives, observing people is one of the most important skills necessary to understand people and communicate with them. The people you are talking to may be perfectly normal people, but often they are doing something unusual. The art of recognising this will often reveal special ideas to you very quickly. *Jeff Goodby: »They are normal people and advertising people have a tendency to treat people in stereo-typical ways, they tend to overlook and to forget that.«*

With regard to the product, what human behaviour could give you a strategic idea?

Develop a Passion for the Situation of the Product User

It is the power of passion and the search for truth, which breaks through superficial marketing bla bla, and leads to new perceptions. It also helps to bring in your own experience with the branch even if they are negative. *Jon Matthews:* »*I try to get passionate as a consumer of that product, so we got passionate about banks. Banks are shit! You charged me for that, you know just because I was overdrawn for two days and had all this money in that account and you didn't transfer it. So you get emotional from a point of view as a consumer.*«

I want to change people's life. I believe that anything you offer has to empower the life of the user.

Abel Reis

Those who only occupy themselves with the one-dimensional view of advertising or the client, will easily lose this meaningful and important perspective.

Abel Reis: »*I want to change people's life. I believe that anything you offer has to empower the life of the user.*«

People are more interesting than products always.

Andrew Cracknell

So it can also be helpful to turn around the entire context and to focus on the people instead of the product. *Andrew Cracknell:* »*Instead of trying to write an ad about that product and how it will fit into people's lives, go write an ad about people and how that product could fit into their lives. Put the emphasis the other way round. People are more interesting than products always.*«

What really gets you excited about this product
and what idea does that give you?

Tell Us a Human Story that Happened

Regardless of what country in the world the idea should be significant for, if it does not have a human touch it will not be relevant. Many of the stories that happen to all of us can be used later, for example, in the McDonald's spot in which a little boy wakes his parents at 3 o'clock in the morning to go to McDonald's. *Jon Moore: »My son actually came in our room at three in the morning completely dressed and wanted to go to his friend's house. I can't believe it happened! I then just put McDonald's in there. The stuff that tends to entertain people are things that have some basis in reality, that you can relate to.«*

Many Top-Creatives keep a kind of diary in order to record their observations and anecdotes, some of which come from childhood. For example: to grab a handkerchief from another person just as he is about to sneeze into it. *Johan Gulbranson: »This story with the handkerchief happened to my stepfather when he was young, so I had it in the book for three or four years and now I can use it. He told me about it once and now I write down funny things in an Idea Book.«*

In what true story could your product play the leading role?

Get in Touch with the Emotional Centre of the Market

Identifying with the brand and its relationship to people is an important basis for the development of an emotional strategy. *Fernando Vega Olmos: »Get in touch with the people and try to understand what they feel, what they love and what they hate. Then, with all this emotion find the best process to put the brand in the core of the emotion of these people.«*

We are 10 per cent rational, and the rest is just emotions.

Fernando Vega Olmos

A lot of energy exists in the emotional centre of human beings, which can be used if you are in some way connected to the product. In order to discover this energy, Top-Creatives place themselves in the emotional user-situation. *Fernando Vega Olmos: »I try to get into the mood. Okay, I'm a housewife, I'm trying to get some product to keep my house clean, what can I feel about this, I hate this work, or I love it, I'm trying to understand this. Because we are 10 per cent rational, and the rest is just emotions.«*

What big emotions in your market are connected to the use of your brand?

Solve a Problem for the Whole Market

The bigger the problem is, the bigger the solution can be. The more you define a specific problem as a general problem, the more people you will reach with this strategy. *Jon Matthews* on the campaign development for a bank: *»We were talking through the planning zone, we said okay this should be about money and the way it interacts with people's lives. It gets you at the centre of the market and if you're there you can do most things.«*

One essential characteristic of a Big Idea is that it can burst boundaries. It reaches more people than the actual target group. So it is often not just a solution for a specific product, but for an entire category. Simply because it offers a relevant message based on a fundamental need.

One example for this is the job for Aspro, in which you see a man giving his wife (who is pretending to have a headache and doesn't want to have sex) a quick-working headache tablet. *John Hunt: »There must be millions of stories about wives or girlfriends who, at a given moment, are not particularly keen on sex. It's a human truth, it's a universal truth, whether you are in*

Italy, Spain or South Africa, and the fun part there was taking that and putting it in an analgesic category.«

What is the biggest common problem you could touch on, and what can your product offer as a solution?

Research the Competitive Advantages of Your Product

The uniqueness of a product arises primarily from the observation and analysis of the competition. The more this uniqueness or advantage is brought out, the easier it will be to develop a strong unique idea from this.

*Jack Mariucci: »**The first thing you want to find out with any client is what their strong points are. If they have an advantage over their competitor you want to attack that advantage. You want to go after that. You want to make that the highlight of the commercial.**«*

You will not always find useful competition information in the well-known or expected areas. *Nick Worthington: »**We often react against stuff and look at what everyone else is doing and then try to do the opposite, or try and move it on to the area where somebody hasn't been yet.**«*

This is not only true for the content of the message, but also for the execution of the idea.

To what new unique message could you summarise the advantages of your product?

Study Competition on the Benefit Level

A strategically defined benefit is often also used in other markets. For instance, the message that something is refreshing is used for peppermint drops, yoghurt, water, soft drinks and even beer. This is because the human motive has a varied effect, depending on the person and the situation.

Xavi Garcias: »The first thing I do is re-compile a lot of information on all the advertising that has been done about this benefit. I look at the competition. I see the good things and the mistakes of people who have already worked on this idea. If I were a lawyer it would be as if I studied all the prior jurisprudence, the other cases and the sentences. Then I choose the best concept transmitting this benefit, and I try to look for a completely new way.«

This high quality confrontation with the anatomy of ideas inspires new ideas. Not only do you look at new images and layouts, as in many award-books, but also strategies and new ways to understand human motives are examined.

How is the benefit of your product communicated in other markets and what can you learn from this?

Observe the Details and Pattern of Life

Great Ideas usually have a strong connection to real life, as it is, or as we would like it to be. Triggers for these ideas can be given by situations that we have experienced ourselves, or from stories we have heard from others. For this purpose, we have to learn to really observe life.
Jeff Goodby: You have to pay attention to what's going on around you, if something is changing, if something is pretty, if there's a pattern to something where there wasn't a pattern before, you should make it your business to notice that.«

Top-Creatives are brilliant observers. They enjoy recognising things others have missed out and use this as a vehicle for their messages.

You have to pay attention to what's going on around you.

Jeff Goodby

Dave Linne: »I'm a kind of voyeur. I really enjoy watching people. I like spying. I like eaves-dropping.«

With this increased awareness in everyday life you will gain important information for new stories and ideas. *Erik Wünsch: »The big companies have to communicate with everyday people and we have to get involved with them. The biggest mistakes that advertising agencies can make is that they lose their grip on society. We always want to be in a people's environment where the real people live.«*

*What message could you attach to a "secret"
or observed detail of your product?*

Use an Event from the Present or Future

Special incidents can also be used for ideas if it is possible to associate them with the product. So Top-Creatives always have their ear to the ground. They know what is in and what is out, and what is currently up to date. *Matthias Freuler: »I try if possible to find an association to some event that is happening during the year. And with the footballer it really was the European Cup and the fact that Switzerland was currently better at football than it had been for over 30 years.«* From this initial thought, the idea of a cow playing football was born for the Swiss

Dairy Association. According to the same principle, a floating cow was developed later because it was the first time a Swiss person was aboard a space station.

Top-Creatives do not always develop strategies and ideas in a straight-line way. They are however, more consistent in using the information available. Similar to a good surfer, they will jump at a current chance and pull everybody along with them with their excitement. *Bob Moore: »I saw the 100-year old marathon runner on the news and grabbed an Art Director I was working with at the same time and showed him the clip from 'This Morning' news show. We came up with an idea and went and showed it to Dan Wieden. Dan said 'great', we showed it to the client and the next week the client said 'great'. We went down there to talk to this 100-year old guy, George Bakewell. He loved it and within a month we had the spot finished.«*

Current events that are bigger than the respective briefing make every idea bigger, and additionally offer a true and attractive association to real life.

Which current event could you associate your Strategy Idea with?

Look at the Strategy Development as a Brain Twister

There is a reason why brain twisters have their fans. With the fastest processor in the world – our brain – we can scan markets and competition environments, and make new differentiated propositions about the product. Regarding thinking as a kind of sport relaxes you and produces a large amount of energy. Many Top-Creatives look at the strategy development from the sport page angle.

Rich Silverstein: »You have to believe that you can solve the problem in a way that nobody else has done it, and that you can out-think anybody.«

*You have to believe that you can solve the problem
in a way that nobody else has done it,*

Rich Silverstein

and that you can out-think anybody.

You should keep your sights on your ambition as a Creative and as an Advisor in the thinking game. If you don't start competitive thinking before you reach the layout level, you will waste a lot of time later, because an idea will become considerably slower as it materialises. And even the best layout cannot compensate for a weak thought.

*How could you describe your strategic assignment
in form of a clever brain twister?*

How to Focus an Energy to Start an Idea:

A good brief

A good Creative Brief sets the basis on which ideas can be sparked off – consciously or subconsciously. It immediately inspires everyone that comes in contact with it. In order to achieve this, the Creative Brief reduces the strategy to its essence. This reduction turns the small light of a torch into a kind of focussed "laser beam", from which many ideas can be sparked off. They implement the strategic message in different ways.

is when you get

excited

Nick Worthington

The Creative Brief Leads the Creative Energy and Focuses it

A good Creative Brief reduces the most important facts to the essentials. It describes the creative strategy that was worked out in the previous work phases, in a very short form, i.e., "brief".

Leaving out unnecessary facts creates a focus from which ideas can be sparked off. *John Hunt: »In the end the brief should have taken all the information and funnelled it for you, so although it can't give you any answers, it can give you a focussed feel to start working.«* This type of focussing requires responsibility and courage, like every idea. This is why you have to place similarly high demands on a good Creative Brief as you do on an idea:

> *A good Creative Brief is, like a strong idea,*
> *simple, relevant and easily understandable.*

A good Creative Brief offers a strategic proposition on a high energy level. This highly condensed and targeted strategic message is in the centre, the "Single-minded Proposition". However, very often this creative focussed energy is split by the desire of the client to have several promises for a product or a service, which can often hinder the birth of Great Ideas.

Top-Creatives concentrate intensively on the formulation of the Creative Brief because they know that a bad Creative Brief can rob, scatter and block energy. People who brief, shorten and steer the thoughts of others in a particular direction. Skilled focussing on a job is therefore a very important inspiration factor, so the creative thought can be lead in the right direction and inspire the creative person.

Rob Kitchen: »If you are not inspired by the nature of the problem they are giving you, then you can't work. Or you can work, but you are not going to come up with anything that's inspirational for them. One of the biggest problems that creative people have, a lot of times, is just not being enthused by the brief.«

In order to ensure an enthusing Creative Brief, Top-Creatives develop ideas in two steps. They differentiate between the direction in which the solution lies (Strategic Idea) and the creative interpre-

tation of this direction (Execution Idea). They consciously divide the task into two parts so that they can solve it quicker, being secure to work on the right inspiring focus point.

*Xavi Garcias: »**The first decision is rational, but the interpretation is very creative. It's like a butterfly and a caterpillar, a metamorphosis. Without caterpillar, there's no butterfly.**«* Is your butterfly on strategy?

As The Creative Brief sets up a mutual work platform, it serves in taking the task off just one person's shoulders and also delivers criteria for a reliable judgement of the idea. That way it prevents a purely subjective evaluation of the idea according to personal preferences and decisions based on taste. »***All creativity is relative in some shape or form. It has got to be relative to something, and the clearest thing it can be relative to is the brief.***«

The more unusual an idea is, the more important a clear strategic evaluation will be. *Loz Simpson:* »***If you don't have a brief how do you judge the work? The work is there to do a job, it's not art, it's business. So if you don't have those parameters, how do you know whether the ad is any good, apart from just gut feel?***"

In order to check whether your Creative Brief provides a clear direction, inspires, and is capable of evaluating whether the idea is on strategy, you can ask yourself:

☆ Does the Creative Brief provide you with a new inspiring perspective of the assignment?
☆ Does its focus contain one clear strategic message, which places a single thought in the centre?
☆ Does the form of this idea inspire you to several other surprising thoughts and ideas and does it give you energy?
☆ Is the Creative Brief a binding and approved work platform, that everybody responsible for the idea (Client, Account Manager, Strategic Planner, Creative Director) knows and has released?

☆ Does your Creative Brief offer a precise and secure basis for the evaluation of the idea later as to whether it is on strategy?

If you can answer these questions with "yes", everybody who reads your Creative Brief will immediately and continuously develop ideas in a very short time, one better than the other. If not however, you do not have a very good work basis. The worst thing is, if you do happen to have a good idea, you will hardly be sure of it, because you do not have any evaluation criteria. And if you do notice it, it will not be any great help either, because you do not have any strategy that you can use to argue for the idea, and defend it in the face of criticism. The following tips will help you to set up a better work platform.

Fight for a Clear Creative Brief

Even though Creatives do receive a briefing or a Creative Brief, many don't check it for quality. A clear briefing contains clear information on what should be communicated and achieved. If you don't know the right direction to go in, you'll get lost.

John Hegarty: »I wouldn't really start to work unless I had a clear brief. My greatest fear is just being told 'have an idea', and you say, well, about what? That isn't the way it works. The way it works is you have an objective of what you are trying to achieve. I need those parameters within which to work. I need a clear brief definitely.«

You won't always automatically receive a clear briefing. Sometimes you have to fight for it. *John Hegarty: »You can always get a clear brief and if you can't, then you have to go and get one. Just decide, don't start working until you have got a clear brief. Who are you talking to? What are the objectives? What do you want people to do as a result of what you have done? That is important, very important.«*

I wouldn't really start to work unless I had a clear brief. My greatest fear is just being told 'have an idea', and you say, well, about what?

John Hegarty

This also means that you should not even begin to work with a bad briefing. Otherwise the danger is that you begin to search for an idea with an irrelevant or maybe even a false work platform.

What information would bring your assignment to the point more clearly?

Make Sure You Really Understand the Assignment Yourself

Just how important it is that the Creative really and truly understands the assignment becomes clear when it comes to speed. *Susan Hoffman: »Make sure you understand what the real assignment is, make sure that you get into your own research in figuring out, understanding it well enough, make sure you are passionate about it, and if it's taking too long there's something wrong.«*

If you don't understand the Creative Brief you will not be able to come up with ideas quickly. So the thought process on which the Creative Brief is based must be substantial and immediately understandable. *Richard Flintham: »We usually ask the people who wrote the brief to come in and talk to us about why they came up with that. We ask to see the client brief that was given to the people who wrote the brief before. We will see those two things. What was a problem, or the opportunity, and then sometimes in the client brief there are really good things to read.«*

Even with all the advantages of Strategic Planning, a lot of important primary information can get lost on the road to certain conclusions. These "tiny information parts" are often triggers for completely new ideas. The more holistically the assignment has been understood, the better the unusual ideas work, as they are secured by facts. *Richard Flintham:* »***The most relevant strategy should give you license to do the most radical ads.***«

What would make the assignment more understandable?

Write a Promise that Immediately Inspires

In many cases the formulation of the assignment is not really inspiring for the Creative. Too often it is just a passing on a short form of briefing information the client has given, which has not yet been condensed, processed or reflected. Since the Creative Brief is the spring-board to find ideas, this spring board should be properly prepared. It should be "exciting" so that you have fun jumping.

If the proposition is good enough in the first place you should be able to do the most creative things imaginable.

Marek Grabowski

You can check if the Creative Brief is really inspiring on the number of solutions that immediately enter your head. *Susan Westre:* »***When an account person comes in with the brief or the problem that you're trying to solve, if I don't have three or four ideas popping into my head as they are talking about it then I don't think they have done a very good job.***«

Energy is also transmitted on a personal level. If a person has not added anything of his own to the assignment he can hardly be excited about the assignment, cannot identify with it, or be really inspiring. *Rob Kitchen:* »*It's very important that the person who is giving the brief is enthusiastic and has researched things inside out so they can answer any questions that you might have at any time.*«

How can you formulate the promise in a more inspiring and exciting way?

Make a "Single-minded Proposition"

If you emphasize everything you emphasise nothing, and if you communicate several promises, they end up being in competition with each other. This means a Creative Brief without a single-minded proposition is a false Creative Brief.

Rob Kitchen: »*If the brief has no single-minded focus, it just goes straight back. It's very important, because otherwise you waste your own time so you produce work to the brief. And if the brief isn't correct, then the work isn't correct. It takes a long time to work out that the brief was wrong. It just wastes everybody's time.*«

Every message focuses our attention, both consciously and subconsciously. The single-minded proposition is therefore the decisive inspiration tool of the Creative Brief. It is the most important base for Great Ideas. *Donna Weinheim:* »*You are setting yourself up for failure if you try to say three things or four things then they will probably end up not remembering anything. You need to convey one message, one thought.*«

When energy or an idea is broken-down, this has an influence on the later stage of the Creative Process. *Alexandra Taylor:* »*If you're not getting somewhere it's usually the brief is wrong, your*

proposition is wrong. Sometimes you are not getting the simplicity of the idea, you're not reaching that point and it's usually because it's too complicated.«

Rob Kitchen

A "simple" proposition does not fall in to your lap automatically and it is worthwhile to remind each other of this and to fight for such a proposition. *Alexandra Taylor: »It's a problem of repeatedly saying it's not good enough, go back, go away, come back.«*

W h a t   i s   t h e   m o s t   i m p o r t a n t   " s i m p l e "   p r o m i s e
t h a t   y o u   w a n t   t o   c o m m u n i c a t e ?

Examine the Relevance of the Promise like a Door-to-Door Salesman

A strong inspiring promise opens doors that were closed before. It allows you direct access to your target group and makes it clear that advertising is a sales job.

Bob Isherwood: »I always think of myself as a door-to-door salesman and I think in terms of headlines like, I knock on the door and someone opens the door and what I have got is a headline, and it is either going to get me inside the door or they'll shut it.«

Sometimes increased access to the target group is based on a new insight, regarding the person who is supposed to open the door. *Gerard Stamp: »It needs a real insight, human insight for a real fact for it to work, and if it hasn't, it's normally just so much hot air. The human insight in the Johnny Walker commercial which is that we're only around once. You've got to live every moment as if it were your last. It's a sentiment we all carry around one way or another, so that's why it strikes a cord with everybody.«*

The more specifically you realise what the message is that reaches people, the more specific and more relevant the ideas inspired by this will be.

What would make your promise to the target group more relevant and surprising?

Shorten Your Promise

Like Great Ideas, Great Promises can be explained in one sentence.

Rob Kitchen: »A single-minded proposition should not be more than six to ten words and then a justification for coming up with that proposition. If you ever see in a proposition a full stop and another sentence, then that's alarm bells, because they are trying to say three things instead of one. This means they haven't actually got to the single core nature of the problem.«

A single-minded proposition should not be
more than six to ten words.

Rob Kitchen

In order to secure such a simple and short message the proposition should be agreed upon with the client. Very often the client wants to say several good things about his product. In doing so he often subconsciously reduces the basis for Great Ideas with regard to the direction of an idea. *Alexandra Taylor: »If the proposition isn't single-minded, if it's confusing, if there's more than*

one way of approaching something, it becomes very difficult, so the thinking at the very beginning is critical to doing great ads.«

Bob Isherwood

If you emphasize everything, you emphasize nothing. *Bob Isherwood:* »**Make sure that you keep it to one message. Because the more you put in the less people take out.**«

What word could you strike from your proposition without losing the meaning or the relevance of its message?

Formulate the Core of the Proposition as an Exciting Question

Questions are more exciting than answers, and we have enough answers around to questions that nobody has ever asked. The transformation of a proposition into an exciting question gives additional energy. *Dan Wieden:* »**The best briefings and the best assignments are trying to figure out what is the question we want to ask, not what is the answer to the question. The best strategy is a well-defined question.**«

With a question we are setting the information flow in motion, we channel the information and control it. It is important however, that it is an exciting question, which should basically fulfil two criteria:

Dan Wieden: »**You don't automatically know the answer to it, and it comes out of the heart of the strategic issue you are trying to deal with.**«

The best strategy is a well-defined question.

Dan Wieden

If we already know the answer, the question is no longer exciting. And if we can't get the question out of the strategic issue, the answer will not be relevant, because already the question itself was not on strategy. *Bob Moore: »It is an art for a planner or an account person to be able to phrase a question in a way that is challenging for a creative person.«*

What is your core message as an exciting question?

Digest the Creative Briefing for a Better Understanding of the Assignment

When we absorb a lot of information we have to digest and filter it. This is a natural process and takes time.

Lee Garfinkel: »I just have as much information as possible, then it would be nice if I could take a day or two to just let it sink in and forget about the stuff that was meaningless and just remember the important information.« Our brain sometimes needs distance from the problem in order to sort out the information. It is not until the actual core has been identified that we can find new approaches on conscious or subconscious levels. *Richard Flintham: »Once they have gone, we'll probably not work on it for a couple of days. Just work on other stuff in your spare moments, just be thinking about this one. It's just nice to give yourself a little bit of space, so that you can digest the brief.«*

Within this process we can move easier from detailed observation to the overall picture, a bigger framework in which we see the assignment and the client with different eyes, so we can interpret

things in a surprising way. *Richard Flintham:* »**It's more having a much bigger, rather than a more particular problem, it's more about having a feeling for the client than the product.**«

It's just nice to give yourself a little bit of space,

Richard Flintham

so that you can digest the brief.

In order to define the space in which the solution is supposed to be, Top-Creatives take their feelings for the client into account. But mostly it is a question of letting the briefing work for itself until it creates a space in which you can work. *Loz Simpson:* »**Read the brief, understand it and then forget about it. Because sometimes things come when you're not thinking about them. They bubble up from your subconscious sometimes.**«

Do you already have enough distance from the problem so you can play with the assignment?

Attack the Creative Brief just like You Attack an Idea

Because the information is condensed and brought to a focus point in a briefing it is important that this point is sufficiently secured. Any unclear thoughts have to be gotten rid of now and agreed upon with the client, otherwise they will consciously or unconsciously continue on into the following phase of finding an idea. *Marcello Serpa:* »**Sometimes the client is so convinced of a particular direction that he subliminally writes it into his (client) briefing. If I am not 100 per cent in agreement with this direction, then I have to stop the whole process before it begins.**«

Unclear thoughts can block the creative process in many different ways. *Marcello Serpa:* »**Most clients have the desire to say everything in 30 seconds and not everything suits. You have to have a focus on something. I discuss this with the client before we begin.**«

Questioning the briefing serves to secure the creative work basis. As long as we are not sure if this basis is correct, the entire coming work stands on shaky ground. Just as a good chef de cuisine, you have to double check if you already have the right ingredients. *Rob Kitchen:* »**When they come up with the brief we ask many questions like: Are you sure about this, is this the right person we are talking to, why not TV, why magazines, why are we talking to housewives, why not children? So these people need to know all the answers.**«

Hansjörg Zürcher

If, in the end, the Creative Brief is regarded as being bad it must be rejected. *Hansjörg Zürcher:* »**The Creatives have the right not to accept a briefing or to say this strategy is bad.**«

How do you know if your Creative Brief has a Great Idea, does it give you energy?

Get the Client to Sign the Creative Brief

The Creative Brief is a binding work basis and later also an evaluation basis for the idea. If a Creative Brief is not signed or approved it will not provide this basis. *Gerard Stamp:* »**The client has to sign the brief, get on board with the brief. Otherwise it's a complete waste of time.**«

The lack of commitment by the client for the Creative Brief will allow him all the freedom later when evaluating the idea. *Hansjörg Zürcher:* »**We want the client to say I will sign this platform, we do not want to go to the client with layouts and storyboards and then a strategy discussion begins.**«

The client has to sign the brief, get on board with the brief. Otherwise it's a complete waste of time.

Gerard Stamp

For this reason make sure that your Creative Brief is also jointly accepted by all of those responsible on the client side.

What percentage of your Creative Brief will be presented to the client and approved by him before you start to find an idea?

How to Receive an Answer that YOU Did not Expect:

Wouldn't

The moment an idea shows up is often experienced as a surprising answer. Surprising, because often we don't know the question that leads to the answer. This makes the coming up with an idea appear to be somewhat mystical. But only with complete openness, when we are not thinking, not evaluating, not knowing, can we build new answers from an apparently meaningless combination of questions. In search of a better question for an even better idea.

it be silly,

if ...

Rob Kitchen

The Finding an Idea as a Surprising New Answer to an Exciting Question

It is the new unusual question that leads to a new unusual answer. Normally, it is not even consciously formulated but more or less subconsciously, or by-the-way. And it happens at the moment, when we least expect it. "What if....?" is probably the best known question of all, to make a new idea, a new question show up.

Assuming that in creative phases such questions are usually asked subconsciously, and the process of finding ideas often runs without our having done anything, Top-Creatives concentrate primarily on absolute openness. *Dan Wieden:* **»It is an affair you are having with something that you cannot see or hear or taste. You're communicating with something and pulling it up out of non-existence into existence.«**

In order to be really open and relaxed in this phase it helps if you are well prepared. Brilliant information will quickly stimulate brilliant questions and new combinations of answers. The strategic proposition in the Creative Brief focuses and fixes the attention on the main point. This allows more openness, which is extremely important at the moment the idea shows up because:

*An idea that shows up is already present
and materialised in another space.*

In order to make it possible that an idea can show up, Top-Creatives provide suitable conditions in "their space". *John Hegarty:* **»It goes back having an open mind. The ideas are all there, they're floating around. There's also something about things that are in the ether, things that are in the atmosphere. It's a weird, wonderful sensation when it happens.«**

The moment the idea shows up also seems to be dependent on the flow situation in which the person finds himself at the time, whether he is travelling in a train, or a car. For this reason sport, air and rail travel, jogging, cycling and driving a motorbike, taking a shower or using the toilet are often described as inspiring locations, because the body is also physically in a flow. *Kevin Drew Davis:* **»When you are tense at work, and things are stressful there is that moment when you have**

to relax your body. I can't tell you how many queer thoughts I have had while standing at the urinal.«

Time spaces are another kind of spaces that influence the moment the idea shows up. If they are too wide they hinder you from focusing on the assignment, if they are too short, they can put pressure on you that block the idea instead of stimulating it.

However, lack of information, strategies and briefings lead to blockades far more frequently than unsuitable spaces.

The most important thing for finding an idea is that an extensive confrontation with the assignment has already taken place, that valid and exciting information is in your hands, and that thinking has been given a direction through the strategy. Only then will you be able to dissolve yourself from the problem playfully and relaxed, which then leads to the solving of the problem.

Such a solution can happen so playfully that several Top-Creatives have described the reception of the energy of an idea as being similar to the principle of a radio. *Marcello Serpa:* »*Sometimes you see the ideas, that are simply in the air and that somebody just grabbed. Theses ideas went through your head at some time, like a radio receiver, the waves are there and if you have a better antenna you will receive them better.*«

Many people associate the feeling you get when you "receive" such an idea with an intensive physical reaction. *Lee Garfinkel:* »*I start to get a tingle, that's it, that's a great spot, so if you don't feel or I don't feel that the work they've presented to gives me that tingle, then I just keep pushing to go in a different direction.*«

Top-Creatives also let themselves be guided by this feeling in the evaluation of ideas, often described as goose pimples, or shivers all over, excitement, an awareness of light, a feeling of truth, an electric impulse, a feeling of warmth, a pulsation and the desire to transform this energy, to

bring the idea to life. All these have a clear association with the force of energy and can be felt physically. This means:

You don't only feel a really Great Idea in your head;
it is an overall physical experience.

John Hegarty: »*It is almost a high when you have a Great Idea. You feel it, you sense it. You feel every nerve ending in your body is alive.*«

This physical feeling helps to recognize the idea and also explains the moment of relaxation we experience when get the re-laxed answer to a question we felt was filled with tension. This relaxation, this high – which some people try to get by taking drugs – appears to be associated with the expansion of your own personal awareness framework. *Matthias Freuler:* »*It is like opening a window through every single level of awareness.*«

Many Top-Creatives also describe the Creative Moment as an awareness of light. *Ramon Roda:* »*It's a moment when nothing else exists. This moment when you see the beginning of the light and you start to control that.*«

Catching the light is the beginning of an idea.

Gilbert Scher: »*Everything seems to be clear. When I get this moment I know I'm going to find a little light and I try to catch it.*«

In order to manage the moment the idea hits you more consciously, you can ask yourself the following questions:

☆ Do you know which specific physical sensation you experience when you become aware of an idea, do you look for the Great Idea until you really get this feeling?

☆ Are you paying enough attention and are you open enough for a moment in time when you do not have to know or be able to do anything?

☆ Are you prepared to become aware of the very short moment an idea shows up, at any time, any place and to hold on to the experience?

☆ Have you prepared sufficient great questions and are you, above all, prepared to hear the apparently meaningless answers to them?

☆ Are you working in a "time-space" or a physical room that helps you to receive the idea and to remain physically in flow yourself?

If you have answered these questions with "yes", you are in good condition to receive several Great Ideas quickly. If not however, maybe you are working on a boring or unspecific strategy or maybe you are even uncertain of the assignment. All of this will make you unnecessarily tense and tie up your attention. A lack of ideas is the result of a lack in preparation. The following tips will stimulate your process at the moment the idea shows up so that you will arrive at your Great Ideas faster and more easily.

Keep Relaxed when You are Looking for an Idea

Particularly when looking for an idea, Creatives can become cramped when they realise that a certain amount of time has passed and they still haven't found a Great Idea. This can be very unproductive for the Creative Moment.

*John Hegarty: »**You have to be relaxed. I don't think Great Ideas come when you are stressed out and tensed up. I think Great Ideas come when you feel things flowing. You let it go. It's a transcendental moment in a way.**«*

With relaxation you can loosen up your "think muscle" and make room for your Creative Flow, remember you could also say: we don't find ideas, they find us if we are open enough to them.

I think Great Ideas come when you feel things flowing.

John Hegarty

Rich Silverstein says: »*It is almost like Zen. If you just relax it's going to come out. It's really relaxation.*«

One possibility to relax yourself is not to spend too long on approaches that are not getting you anywhere. Stay with the flow and avoid becoming fixated on one idea that has only little potential. *Nick Worthington:* »*If you couldn't think of an idea in half an hour, just cross it off, never go back to it, go on to the next one.*«

How can you turn off typical distracting factors and tensions or reduce them?

Examine what is Wrong when You can't Think of an Idea Quickly

Ideas appear within a nanosecond if the assignment and/or the problem has been prepared sufficiently and formulated in an exciting way. The Creative Brief should inspire you quickly, and if it doesn't it's a sign that something is wrong. *Karel Beyen:* »*I would say don't work longer than ten minutes.*«

Speed is a criterion by which we can see if energy can flow uninfluenced and uninhibitedly. If gaining an idea stumbles or stutters, something is in the way – often it's us. So speed is also a criterion for quality. *Bob Isherwood:* »*I work on the basis that if I can't solve it by lunch time I probably won't solve it that day.*«

Get used to the fact that ideas happen quickly and when you have absolutely no idea something is wrong. If the material that an idea is made up of is pure energy, similar to light, then your ideas

It doesn't take five seconds, it takes a tenth
                                    Loz Simpson
of second to pop in, it's instant.

should happen with the speed of light. *Loz Simpson:* »*It doesn't take five seconds, it takes a tenth of second to pop in, it's instant.*«

What is missing or blocking?
Rely on your first impulse and change this.

Play Instead of Work

Different rules apply to the different phases of the Creative Process. After they have worked hard on the Creative Brief and the Strategy, Top-Creatives start looking for an idea to show up in a playful way. *Marcello Serpa:* »*If I have to suffer then the idea is not good. I don't worry too much about 'I have to sweat', if that is the case I stop immediately. If an idea is good then it happens simply.*«

The true art of finding ideas is to interrupt the analytic process and to forget the hard facts. *Marcello Serpa:* » *At that moment when I have all the information, the real hard facts, the hardware, I throw everything out of my head and begin to fantasise and if nothing happens I stop and do something else.*«

This playful treatment of thoughts avoids blockades and builds an almost childlike openness in all directions for new perspectives and new ideas. *Matthias Freuler:* »*I think the best Creatives are those people who never really grew up. Something which everyone has had in childhood they have managed to hold on to as they got older over the years.*«

Let the inner child in you work. It's a part in you that doesn't censor or rationalise whether something is important or unimportant. *Dan Wieden:* »**Just from the sense of play, you know, if it feels like play, energy is abundant, if it feels like work, oh boy, it is heavy.**«

What would make your work more playful and easier?

Find "Your Own" Concentrated Relaxed Condition

When we concentrate on something and become completely caught up in it, we quickly forget time. *Anette Scholz:* »**You have to be able to build up a world of your own or in a world with the people with whom you are sitting. The concentration must be so strong that you no longer notice your 'surroundings'.**«

In order to absorb new information it appears we have to leave our subjective time space in order to make contact with another level. *Dave Linne:* »**If you're focussed on something, there can be a fire going on in the other part of the room and you don't care. You are not thinking about lunch. Where as if you are not focussed, you're asking, what did we have for lunch today?**«

The concentration must be so strong that you no longer notice your 'surroundings'.

Anette Scholz

This time space in which we can concentrate appears to be limited. *Gilbert Scher:* »**The most important thing for the creative is the concentration. It is very hard to get this concentration and I think in a day maybe we get thirtyfive minutes.**«

Jeff Goodby expands: »*In a lot of cases, when I'm able to bring some kind of creative spirit to something, it's usually because I have got myself into the middle of the situation and thought about it through the eyes of the people that are going to watch it.*«

Get through to your inner self, bring the assignment to mind again and relax in order to start the game. Do without everything that will divert your energy, allow for positive stimulation only.

Where can you find a room or space you can best concentrate in?

Retreat into a Quiet "Clean" Room

Distractions divert energy and as a result, divert ideas. For this reason, several Top-Creatives prefer to work alone during some work phases or to go to a far off room for at least part of the time. *Lars Bastholm: »You learn to do what seals do – they close their ears, so I just close my ears and then I'm in my own little space.*«

In order to avoid stress and distractions, several Top-Creatives prefer to work in very neat and tidy rooms. *Kevin Drew Davis: »I am really sensitive to noises around me and to clutter. I try to make a clean and quiet space to think. My door is open 90% of the time but when it is time to think I close the door and make it quiet.*«

The fact that things are in order is a perfect moment for me to begin the creative process.

Juan Gallardo

Others use the tidying up time to get into a relaxed mode. *Juan Gallardo: »Clearing things up helps me to get organized and it helps the thinking process just by moving things around. Some-*

times I don't even think about it. The fact that things are in order is a perfect moment for me to begin the creative process.«

Such quiet and relaxed places exist in moments when work is absent, when you are no longer thinking of the assignment. *Kevin Drew Davis:* »*A lot of ideas come when I am doing something completely unrelated to work, and that is usually when things sort of hit me.«*

In what place can you relax and think without being disturbed, or how can you set up such a space?

Change Your Perspective – Physically

When we are concentrating heavily our bodies can become tense as well. On the other hand, a change in the physical position automatically leads to a change in your mental state, because new perspectives always also lead to a change in input. *John Hegarty:* »*I always say to creatives when you're stuck with a problem change seats. You will see a different wall with different things on it and all of a sudden your mind will be sparked off in a different direction. Keep changing things, keep altering, keep moving around, keep that mind open.«*

John Hegarty

Many Top-Creative have also experienced this bodily stimulus, physically, as a flow – when travelling, at sport or when they change from one status quo to another. *Jeff Goodby:* »*I can think about something just before I fall asleep, and then when I wake up it's kind of organised in my*

head and I can just sit down and write it down. It all organises itself while I'm asleep, which is pretty helpful.«

Letting go off the known perspective leads to new insights automatically, in every phase. *Johan Gulbranson: »Usually when I do a commercial the first ideas you get, everybody gets, it is so obvious, so you have to find another point of view, to see from another angle. I try to find from which angle I should tell it.«*

What perspective would provide completely new insights to your assignment?

Work in a Place that Relaxes You

The more relaxed you are, the easier it will be for the idea to find its way to you. *Nick Worthington: »It just takes a second to think of a Great Idea, but you have to give yourself the space to have that idea. Allow the chance of that idea to happen. You start off with your preconceptions about the product by thought-of-process, not discovery, and then you arrive at a more educated sort of place. That's when you can do an ad.«*

Top-Creatives are extremely aware of the atmosphere of surroundings that allows them to concentrate on the assignment and develop new, revolutionary ideas. *Gilbert Scher: »All my best work I did at home because I think it's important to work in an environment which is pleasant. I like to work with books, music, my wallpaper and my desk. I am aware that I am quiet, I am comfortable and totally on the question.«*

These conditions should also be set up in the Creative Department. *Rob Kitchen: »An atmosphere in the creative department is very important. It should be nice and relaxed and you should be free to be able to say what you like to whoever you like. You shouldn't be afraid of opening a door.«*

Many Top-Creatives also deliberately use these creative, stimulating and open kind of conditions in the toilet, the bathtub, under the shower, when going for a walk, yes, even at sports or riding a motorbike, in tune and in harmony with themselves. *Toni Segarra: »I have a lot of ideas out of the agency at the cinema, the bar, my home, in the shower. The moment the concept becomes an idea, a form, the moment when everything goes click and it comes together, is the moment you are not thinking about it.« Paul Spencer: »I run a lot. During the run I find all kinds of stuff.«*

I like to work with books, music,

Gilbert Scher

my wallpaper and my desk.

For the boss of an agency the design of a Creative Room is determined by completely different forces. *Lee Garfinkel: »I realised pretty early that I'm much more relaxed wearing T-Shirts and jeans, it's easier for me to think than to have a shirt and tie and feel all stiff.«*

What surroundings in a room help you to relax?

Work Very Early in the Morning

As a space in which ideas can happen, the space of time also plays an important role. Top-Creatives like to work in the future before others get there. *John Hegarty: »I like being ahead and I always sense that if I start early, I'm ahead. I get that feeling that I'm in front of things rather than if I start late.«*

For many, very early in the morning, the day doesn't start in the agency. *Jeff Goodby: »I work in the morning a lot. I wake up at 5 o'clock, I go down to my basement where my studio is set up and I work there.«*

Mike Wells: »I get up about 6 and often come in here about 7:30. I find that's a very peaceful time.«

Marcello Siqueira: »From midnight to 5 o'clock in the morning is the best time for me.«

Every distraction of concentration on the assignment, and as a result, unnecessary burning up of your own energy is regarded as a disturbance. *Michael Patti: »I am best on Saturdays with my partner, alone in the office, no one is around, no phone is ringing, nobody is asking me questions.«*

I get up at seven. I prepare my day.
It's like a football player. You can't win matches
without training. Being in the office is the match.
From seven to ten I train.

Xavi Garcias

In particular, an undisturbed, quiet atmosphere promotes creative concentration; of course, several Top-Creatives also find this in the late evening. However, many of them feel fresher in the morning and full of energy, and are as such, ahead of the daily trot.

Xavi Garcias: »I get up at seven. I prepare my day. It's like a football player. You can't win matches without training. Being in the office is the match. From seven to ten I train.«

What quiet time-spaces have you never worked in?

Produce Masses, in Order to have Choices

The strategic message, the single-minded proposition, can be widely interpreted. A quick trial of shades, possibilities and forms, does not only produce a flow condition and relaxes you, but also allows you to select the best of all forms for realisation, from several different solutions. For this reason for Top-Creatives, quality is generated through the quantity of ideas. *Marcello Serpa:* »*I sketched 40 pieces of work, out of these I presented 20, and then 8 were approved. Of these only 2 were briefed. I always do quantity, I have to do an enormous amount, I can't do one ad and say that's it, I do 30 to 40.*« This method of working also makes the selected idea safer at the presentation.

Nick Worthington: »*If you only do ten pieces of work then you're going to have one piece of good work to your name. But if you do 100 pieces, you're going to have ten good pieces to your name and then you're not a crap advertiser anymore.*«

Marcello Serpa

For the Mercedes SLK poster "Skid marks", that received the Grand-Prix award in Cannes, also far more pieces than the desired launch theme were produced. *Gerard Stamp:* »*Dozens and dozens were produced, most of which were not really good, most were just rubbish, but one or two were quite good. There must have been 40 or 50 or so altogether.*«

Don Schneider: »*Our kill rate is about 30 to 1. We write about 30 commercials for a keeper, something like that.*« In order to produce this mass amount it is of course necessary to work quickly, to switch over to scribbles instead of producing deeply executed ideas. And if you are working in a playful manner you won't have any problem with the mass production. Just play more and faster!

How many ideas do you develop for a solution, 20, 50, 100?

84 Produce Masses for Relaxation

Quantity not only produces a choice but also relaxes you, because you know that you have already produced a meaningful amount of ideas. *Paul Spencer:* »*I often find my best individual ads or commercials are the last one of the group, you didn't care any more, you already had it so you felt free.*«

Also, the rejection of ideas is a more natural thing for somebody that has already produced masses. *Richard Flintham:* »*Say twenty scripts that are rejected to get one bought. We used to go in and one of them would go forward, because there can only be one sold. We are used to rejection at a very early stage in the creative department.*«

I often find my best individual ads or commercials
are the last one of the group, you didn't care any more,
you already had it so you felt free.

Paul Spencer

If you only have 2 ideas, the rejection will hit you at 50 per cent. If you have 20 however, the rejection of each individual idea is of less importance. 19 rejections are, at the same time, 19 enforcements of the 20th idea. The principle of rejection also holds true at another level. *Marcello Serpa:* »*With ideas it is the same as with sperms, they are all in the running and one makes it, that's*

why I don't kill any of them. Ideas that are halfway good get to take part in the running, and if one of them is strong enough it will get through to the end.«

In the following concept mass production also appears to be an important factor and allows choices that relax you. *Nick Worthington:* »*A friend of ours at college used to get off with lots and lots of girls all the time, and we never got off with any. And he said, 'look, you know what's your problem? You ask one girl a year if she wants to go out with you, and she says no, and then you don't ask anyone for another year. Then you build up the courage to ask another girl out, and you do it and she says no, and then you wait another year, and you wait another year before you ask someone else. I ask ten girls a night and I always get one'.*«

How many good ideas do you need to be relaxed when finding an idea?

Be Open for the Ideas around You

Openness is important to pick up new information, to increase awareness of ideas, but also for the interpretation of the idea. This mental openness is strongly recommended by Top-Creatives. *John Hegarty:* »*I just read as much as I possibly can, see as much as I possibly can, keep my mind as open as I possibly can to as many things, and I think through that you become a better creative person. I like experimenting. I just like the idea of constant change. I don't like to feel that 'this is it', that routine is something which bothers me.*«

You know where the idea is, but you have to sweep your mind to the left and the right and then you say ah, it's here. You have to look for the idea.

Gilbert Scher

In order for an idea to be caught, it must already exist. If we assume that ideas already exist, the process of the search for the idea also changes, because we are not looking for something that doesn't exist, but for something that is already there, we just have to make it visible. *Gilbert Scher:* »*You know where the idea is, but you have to sweep your mind to the left and the right and then you say ah, it's here. You have to look for the idea.*« Being creative in effect means turning something that already exists into something obvious visible for other people.

How can you change your surroundings so the ideas around you can show up easier?

Start off Alone with the Processing of the Assignment

It is very effective to explore the fundamental assignment yourself. First of all, because when your standards are very high, many ideas in the beginning are simply not good enough.

Silverstein and I work traditionally in spurts.

Jeff Goodby

Steve Simpson: »*I think there's a creative phase that has to be completely uninhibited. Because for every fairly decent idea you have ten really bad ones. I find it useful to have at least an idea or a thought about a problem before I start talking to other people about it.*«

Individual work styles also allow for new approaches to the idea. *Nick Worthington:* »*We almost work independently from each other. We'll talk about stuff a lot and we'll talk to other people a lot about it. He'll go off and look at stuff and I'll go off and look at stuff independently, and then we will work on it, and pump out as many ideas as we can.*«

A good team makes this possible, but also doubles the output of ideas. *Matthias Freuler: »I sit myself down all on my own and start to study. Then the Art Director joins me, we put the first ideas together and later we have twice as many ideas and together we come up with something.«*

Brainstormings aren't just for saying whatever comes to mind, you have to go to them prepared, with something to say.

Xavi Garcias

Far too often we rely on the others, without playing our part in the process. *Xavi Garcias: »Brainstormings aren't just for saying whatever comes to mind, you have to go to them prepared, with something to say. The individual attitude before the group must be good.«*

Many successful agencies have therefore been founded by team partners that still work along these lines. *Jeff Goodby: »Silverstein and I work traditionally in spurts. We sit together for a few minutes, and then we separate and he works on his own and I work on my own, and then we come back together and kind of compare notes.«*

How well do you prepare yourself alone and independently to make an idea show up, or for the brainstorming?

Be Clueless and Empty

When we were kids we asked questions that we didn't think were dumb. We hadn't a clue, today many times we are afraid to ask certain questions, because we are full of knowledge. *Dan Wieden: »To be stupid is an extremely valuable tool, to be innocent and to be open for everything.«*

While a huge amount of information from different areas is absorbed when preparing, for the idea to show up you have to be able to forget this information in order to come up a with a completely new perspective on already existing things.

You need to get rid of all that and approach it
Dan Wieden
new and innocent, that's the most important thing.

Dan Wieden: »*When you begin a piece of work, it is absolutely essential that you somehow rinse your brain about everything you think you know about that project, of that subject, and somehow realise how ignorant you are and how stuffed you are with preconceptions about things. You need to get rid of all that and approach it new and innocent, that's the most important thing.*«

Too much knowledge often hinders the access to new possibilities. We learn and know much about what's just not possible, as we get older. In order to "have a screw loose" we should do away with mental constipation – for instance prejudices – that really limit our awareness.

Which of your greatest convictions could stand
in the way of you having a Great Idea?

Take the Idea Finding Nice and Easy

If you feel that you are totally and completely responsible for solving a problem you will find it very difficult to do so. Many Top-Creatives have therefore compared fishing to the relaxed behaviour when looking for an idea to show up, where there is an aim, but the responsibility to achieve this aim is not totally in the hands of the fisherman.

Don Schneider: »*It's a little bit like fishing, waiting, talking, having a beer and that thing. You know there's something there, you know you have got something that day, it's real. It's a little like fishing, it's like getting a tug from somewhere down in there.*«

Loz Simpson

Just as we cannot force a fish to bite, we cannot force an idea to come to us. Not one form of tension will accelerate the process, on the contrary, it just makes it more uncomfortable. Have you ever seen a stressed out fisherman? The moment the idea shows up, when the fish bites, is more of a meditative, flowing away from reality type of moment, usually when we least expect it. *Paul Spencer:* »*There's a certain Zen quality to all that stuff.*«

In order to have such a Zen quality in daily business, Top-Creatives don't take advertising all too seriously. That also relaxes unbelievably. *Loz Simpson:* »*Not taking it seriously, it's only advertising, it's not really all that important.*«

What do you have to personally believe about an Idea showing up that will let you feel it's easy to do?

Have the Courage to Lose Control

At the moment an idea shows up we seem to be separate from ourselves, free from our own ego. This conscious removal from a purely personal dimension seems to increase the connection of possibilities. *David Caballero:* »*You have to be able to separate yourself from the idea. When I'm concentrating I forget about myself. I'm imagining a spot or an advertisement and then I get into this and I understand what I'm feeling. I have got to make an effort to see this image ... my own language, my own reflections ... for one moment I'm a receiver, I just receive.«*

This also means that you have to have the courage to lose control and just to be, to flow. *David Caballero: »Referring to this creative system, you can take information and that becomes transformed into something else that you very often can't control. You are using intuition and sometimes things come up that you can't quite understand where they came from.«*

The aim is to arrive at a point in which you are as flowing and flighty as the idea. And the more you reduce your "personal resistance", the easier it will be for ideas to flow to you. *Dan Wieden: »Well, it's like being in the 'zone', athletes will talk about being in the 'zone' where all this stuff is interrelated ... all your questions end up coming back to the very same issue, so I end up using the same words and same analogies ... but it's when you are less there and something is working through you, it's very simple and very easy, and when you are present, and strongly present, not much seems to happen.«*

Usually it is your own ego that "blocks" you and you should let it slip into the background, if you want to create new things.

Where and when is it most easy for you to give up control?

Demand the Right to make Mistakes

It is impossible to create a Great Idea, to move into completely new territory and to be completely confident about the results at the same time. *Jack Mariucci: »Taking the risks and failing is important. I would rather fail for attempting to do something different, than just do constantly mediocre work.«*

A creative who doesn't make mistakes,
is not a good creative.

Xavi Garcias

The road to great work leads you automatically to "mis-takes", because you may have taken something, that does not yet make sense. Use these mistakes to get closer to the area where the idea is, because many revolutionary inventions came up from mistakes. *Simon Waterfall: »**The currency of creativity is failure.**«* Actively allowing yourself to make mistakes and accepting the associated risks is the only possibility to develop yourself consciously. Provided that you learn from your mistakes.

*Xavi Garcias: »**A creative who doesn't make mistakes, is not a good creative. One must make mistakes and try to look for the impossible. Not only conform to what you know to be true. I have learned more from my mistakes than from my success.**«*

I would rather fail for attempting to do something different,
than just do constantly mediocre work.

Jack Mariucci

Mistakes are part of being creative. If you accept this it is easier to take risks. Risks are nothing other than situations where we are not sure how they will turn out. This is also true for Great Ideas. If you are not afraid of ideas, you will be more willing to take risks, to explore new territories. *Mike Wells: »**You have to be prepared to make a mistake, otherwise you'll never do anything new or different. Some of the biggest names in the business have made some of the biggest mistakes you can possibly think of.**«*

What mistakes do you fear the most
and how could you overcome this fear?

Say and Write Meaningless Stuff

Meaningful ideas are often very close to nonsense ideas. When coming up with ideas, you shouldn't control yourself too much and allow meaningless stuff to be said, because especially stupid thoughts can stimulate you and help you to arrive at good ideas.

Nick Worthington: »Many people, even if they had for a flash of a moment thought that this was exciting, might just be embarrassed to mention it, don't want to say it, or just convince themselves that it's not good. When you're working, it's really important not to be inhibited, and it comes with experience.«

This limitation of thought is always your own personal responsibility. *Karel Beyen: »Nobody else can mess up your mind, only you can do that.«*

What thoughts and evaluations stop you from writing or saying "meaningless" things?

Have a Typestorming instead of Brainstorming

Very often you lose valuable time when you want to call together all participants and coordinate a brainstorming. Just do it on your own, have a typestorming: just let your thoughts flow into the computer or onto a piece of paper, just type whatever comes into your mind.

Steve Simpson: »I think you shouldn't allow yourself to ask a lot of questions about it. You just have to type. Then the next phase comes afterwards and then you ask: 'Is this true? Does it sound true? Is it interesting? Is it unique in the category or in advertising in general?' Those are the standards that you have to apply to your own work.«

It makes sense to separate the Creative Process from the Evaluation Process. If however, you do not completely separate the Find an Idea phase from the Idea Evaluation phase you will find it very difficult to get into the flow. If we use the rational side of our brain to control our creativity, in a car it would be like putting the brakes on at the same time when you are accelerating the car.

You shouldn't allow yourself to ask a lot of questions about it.

Steve Simpson

A further advantage of typestorming is that you would not have to hold on to an idea in your head for longer, like in some brainstorming, when nobody wants to put it down on paper. *Mike Wells: »You've got to empty your thoughts onto a piece of paper and that allows other thoughts to come. If you leave it in your mind, it just stagnates there. It goes round and round and round and it won't let another idea come out.«*

Such a typestorming can even have meditative characteristics. *Dan Wieden: »It's just like fishing ... you just start writing ... it's like free association, it's like Hemingway sharpening pencils or something, it's like a way of getting in a rhythm or getting free of something. I used to just begin by writing nonsense, just like a stream of consciousness to get by the critic in you that was always trying to edit things and make things logical, sensible. You just lock that guy up in the closet for a while and just type.«*

How can you hold on to your thought-flow better and even quicker?

Just Look at One Aspect of the Message

An attachment to one aspect of the problem ensures that the result is still tied to the assignment. As a human being we have only one attention span. For this reason, reduce your assignment, your

problem or your proposition to a key word. *Rob Kitchen:* »**One of the systems that I have when I'm stuck, is just to write down all the words that occur to me that are to do with one aspect of the problem. Like 'car stuck to the poster'. A lot of words that are associated with cars and then other words that are associated with poster, or the location of the thing. And then I see if there's a pattern.**«

This was also the basis for two brilliant pieces of work. The first one for Araldite glue whose gluing power was proved by gluing a real car to a poster wall. *Rob Kitchen:* »**I was just going through all of the things that one normally uses glue for, and the most banal of all, for English people is the handle always comes off teapots. It doesn't actually, but people think that they do.**«

The second piece of work is for Boddington Beer, in which a pint of beer was alienated in the form of an ice cream or shaving cream. *Mike Wells:* »**The brief was a smooth pint, we interpreted that to mean 'cream', it was a creamy pint. That does come totally out of the product. It's a very creamy pint.**« Such trigger words can come from outside, from the problem, the application, the awareness or directly from the product.

What single aspect of the product or in the proposition leads to completely new associations?

Use Obvious Associations

To be associated means to be connected to something. This means that associations are connections to imaginative thoughts that already exist, that we can use for the idea. *Marcello Serpa:* »**It should be obvious, but so obvious that nobody sees it. And lots of my pieces of work are so obvious.**« An aluminium tin can for instance provide an association to an Audi made of aluminium. *Marcello Serpa:* »**I evaluate whatever you associate with this product. If you associate it with something that already exists, and nobody has done it before, then that's it.**«

For me good advertising is evident.

Marcello Serpa

The perception of what is "evident" but is still not perceived by others, is yet again an indication, that training our powers of perception plays a considerable role in the discovery, revealing and seeing of new ideas and associations. *Marcello Serpa:* **»Other Creatives try to make the things so complicated, in order to make them unique, so that nobody understands the ad later. For me good advertising is evident.«**

If you associate it with something that already exists, and nobody has done it before, then that's it.

Marcello Serpa

Gilbert Scher expresses this with a quotation from the French philosopher Descartes: **»Intuition is something abstract, and in spite of this abstraction intuition is to put an object in clear light of the evidence.«** The word evidence describes a clear and strong energetic connection of an idea that already exists but only needs to be recognized.

Which existing and obvious association can you use for a new exciting idea?

Assume that there Already is a Good Connection

The basic assumption that everything is connected with each other makes it easier for Top-Creatives to make unusual combinations visible. *Felix de Castro* on his work for the Spanish Cancer Association: **»I thought there was probably a link to be used in that fact that women go to the** *beach and take off their tops without any problem, but women don't go to the doctor and take off their tops so the doctor can see their breasts regularly. So there's an interesting contradiction there that could be put together in an ad.«*

Nick Worthington: *»It's nearly always about putting two things together which you're not supposed to have together, or don't usually go together, or don't fit.«*

Similar to a puzzle where the "missing link" is still not there but has already been produced, the assumption that the missing connection already exists is of great help. It also helps us subconsciously to concentrate on the missing piece. In order to produce such a new connection, it is important that we have fundamentally occupied ourselves with the product beforehand.

To which completely different kind of area does a connection or an association definitely exist?

Exaggerate Your "What If" Question

"What if" questions work in all work areas to come up with new ideas. They are important in order to form the first seed of thought, to overcome blockades and to produce new relationships. The question "what if" is an invitation to this.

Ted Sann: *»For me, it's a bit of like finding an area.«*

This area for example was found for a Pepsi Commercial with the following question. *Ted Sann: »What if Coke were dead? How do you express that? I just came up with a notion of a civilisation later on in time, where somebody finds the Coke bottle and nobody has any idea what it is.«*

Jon Moore: »For me it is a process of connecting things, it's like you're taking different bits and kind of connecting them over in your head and saying what if this happened or what if that happened?« Donna Weinheim *tells a similar story: »For the boy in the bottle I had a vision of a little boy on the Jersey shore. I started with that picture, just drinking this bottle of Pepsi. From there it evolved into what would happen if he didn't stop.«*

What exaggerating question would make your idea
even more unusual?

Make Fun of the Problem

To make fun of things and to take them lightly, is another way to cross over borders and discover new things. *Nick Worthington: »If you are having fun and having a bit of a laugh, then ideas just come out.«*

Just as a good joke gives us energy because it offers us an unexpected perception, ideas also give us energy because they show us something new. Even the intentional production of stupid ideas overcomes rational benchmarks and leaves us open for irrational things. *Rob Kitchen: »We knew we had to think about something, and a silly idea just came up ... wouldn't it be silly if ... and it's not so silly ... so that's how it can happen.«*

It is often easier to start with a stupid idea as a basis which will then be tamed, than to start with a normal message that is then supposed to go "crazy". The formulation "what if ...?" produces new connections and associations, for example of the British Intercity. *Rob Kitchen: »What if a business man gets up in the morning, says goodbye to his wife on the doorstep and goes to the garage, opens it and there's a train in it instead of a car?«* The consequences of this "stupid setting" can almost be called logical and will easily bring up completely new aspects of that idea.

By the way, that's why it's especially important not to make fun of new ideas in the early phase of their existence. If you make fun of a difficult problem you are making it lighter. But if you make fun of an idea that is light anyway, it can become even too light and quickly disappear. And who wants to work with an idea that has been made fun of?

With what idea could you make fun
of the core problem of your assignment?

Inspire Yourself with Other Jobs

Also doing work for other clients is a welcome change, so that you don't become blocked on one single job. Different jobs also offer different associations. *Susan Hoffman: »What I actually need is a lot of different work to work on because I like to bounce, and if you gave me one project for a full week that would be really hard. Your mind doesn't work that way, I like the juggle in my brain a little. Here we always have more work than we can do, so it's just the style of working that we've developed.«*

Susan Hoffman

The fact that this way of working also affects the agency system and the work culture is not surprising. In a creative culture, where creative work has priority, more creative work is simultaneously both food and a result of this culture. *Susan Hoffman: »Dan (Wieden) and David (Kennedy) have always felt, and they are right, that creatives are a lot happier when they are overworked. I think when you are underworked you're bored.«*

This type of stimulation only arises in a system where work has the highest priority, and not political persuasions. In this case more work is more fun. And courage and the passion to discover will not be blocked by fear, frustration or ignorance. So that the individual in the system can profit from several inspiring jobs, the system itself has to be inspiring.

What other projects or products could you voluntarily and additionally work on?

Look for Your Dream-Team-Partner

The finding of an idea can also be boosted by an inspiring partner combination. Since team partners complement each other, in good teams the ideas will be bigger. From 2 by 2 you get 5 in this case. Far too often, however, the teams are built too superficially according to personal preferences, instead of performance abilities.

Alexandra Taylor: »You have got to work together with somebody who is as good as yourself if not better. I feel that is one of the main things.«

Rob Kitchen

Usually the best balance is someone who is very confident and someone who is a little bit quieter.

A demanding team partner that you look up to, also gives you reliable orientation, whether an idea is already very good. Working with someone who is "better" also means working with someone who is "different". For this reason team partners that have varying concepts of life make up a good combination. They have a larger pool of different input that is valuable for new ideas.

Nick Worthington: »I think we (Nick Worthington & John Gorse) probably do compliment each other quite well. We share the same sort of goals, but we probably have different routes of getting there. I'm more methodical in the way I work, and a bit more logical. I'll start from some under-standing I've got of something and try to talk to people, get other people's opinions, get a bit of understanding of what's going on. So I have got a strong base. John is more inspired in a way than myself.«

It is exactly the opposite characteristics in a team that can lead to a fantastic compliment of each other.

*You have got to work together with somebody
who is as good as yourself if not better.*

Alexandra Taylor

I feel that is one of the main things.

Rob Kitchen: »That's why I think creative people tend to change partners quite a lot. Because you just don't have that magic meshing of character. Usually the best balance is someone who is very confident and someone who is a little bit quieter.«

So it's often worthwhile for the Creative Director to switch his teams around until the right combi-nation has been found. The partners of well known Top-Creative Teams also had to find each other. Just like you have to use different combinations when trying to make an idea show up, you can also use "what if ...?" in the search for your Dream Team.

Which other partner constellation could you try out?

Look for a Partner with Opposite Characteristics

Opposites attract because they compliment each other. Complementing each other also provides an important condition for the protection of ideas in top teams.

Alexandra Taylor: »If you are both too similar, the chemistry would be no good because you wouldn't be producing great work. What my partner forgets I remember, and what I forget he remembers, so we work very well in that sense of producing great work.«

Lode Schaeffer

Many Top-Creative-Teams stress that regardless of all of their differences they always arrive at a mutual strong conviction in order to protect the idea. *Erik Wünsch* about himself and *Lode Schaeffer: »Everybody treats us as one person and as somebody once said: Without me nobody would hear Erik but without Erik nobody would listen to me.«*

What characteristics has your partner got that balance yours out?

Relax Yourself and Your Partner with Insults

The object of every Creative Team is to mutually define the highest possible standard. One possibility to build up and inspire this standard, is to challenge each other and argue. For some teams this is almost a symbolic act at the beginning of the work.

Michael Patti: »It makes you relax when both partners are going 'You stink, you're horrible, you'll never come up with another idea', you relax because you know that the two of you can work it out. It's just like an exercise you go through.«

You've got to feel very comfortable with your partner
Alexandra Taylor
to be allowed to look silly and foolish, or crazy or mad.

The important thing is that the partnership is stable enough and that every member of the team feels relaxed enough to deal with these familiar insults. *Edwin Veelo: »Teamwork is very fragile, you have to learn how to do but once you do it its awesome, it's the only way to work.«*

Of course the idea is not to really insult each other, but to take the freedom of allowing all the ideas, that are normal to pass one by, so that sometime during this flow, an unusual idea will show up. *Alexandra Taylor: »You've got to feel very comfortable with your partner to be allowed to look silly and foolish, or crazy or mad.«*

Would your partner seriously insult you?
Then change to another.

Look for Your Stimulus Outside of Creative Award Books

Many Creatives orientate themselves on advertising that already exists. The thing is, that new fresh influences can only be found outside of advertising. This may be the explanation why there are so many cliché types of ideas where we have the feeling we have seen them a thousand times before. Reading annuals means you are experiencing second hand creativity. The stuff that ideas are made of can't be found in annuals, but in life itself.

John Hegarty: »**Do interesting things and interesting things will happen to you.**«

In addition, creative annuals are potentially dangerous. *Matthias Freuler:* »**I read very little professional literature, i.e. very little ADC-Books. It is always very dangerous to read those things. Even if you don't consciously want to steal something, if you look at 100 or 200 super ads in a short space of time, something always remains in your head. And one day, when you are looking for an idea, you recall this or that. Perhaps subconsciously.**«

Rich Silverstein says: »**I have never been a student of advertising. I don't look at publications. I don't read Ad-Week. I don't read Advertising Age. When I see creative advertising magazines, I go: 'oh' and put it away. I don't want to get my stimulus from the industry. My cat gives me good ideas.**«

What would immediately make your work more stimulating?

Collect Ideas like a Professional

Great Ideas are energy for companies, brands and products. Many Top-Creatives use the energy of "killed ideas" for other clients.

Everything in life is timing. The right idea won't get done unless it's the right time and the client's in the right mood.

Dave Linne

Dave Linne: »**You never really throw anything away. You always kinda keep ideas, cause a good idea is a good idea. You know, if that spot hadn't sold for Pepsi with the guy, the announcer yelling 'goal', we would have tried it for something else down the road, where it would have been**

right for.« There is a simple reason why you have to conserve good ideas. *David Linne: »Everything in life is timing. The right idea won't get done unless it's the right time and the client's in the right mood.«*

For this reason Top-Creatives collect these ideas in a specially prepared archive or book. *Rob Kitchen: »Smart people don't throw those ideas away. They write them down and put them in a drawer because it will be useful for some other time.«*

> *For which other product, brand or branch could your latest killed idea work as well?*

Always have a Notepad with You

In order to allow the seed of the idea to form at an early stage, it is sometimes worthwhile to just let the idea flow. *Donna Weinheim: »I don't think of an idea and write a script, I jot down about 50 ideas, I just jot them down as notes, I carry a notebook with me wherever I go.«*

Mike Wells: »I always carry tiny little notebooks. I keep them beside my bed because in the middle of the night, and it's frightening, I will suddenly start thinking of ads.«

You should also be prepared to record your thoughts when you are relaxing or just before you fall asleep. *Mike Wells: »It can only take one moment to think of a very exciting idea. You have to be ready when they pop along.«*

The energy from an idea can also be very pushy. It doesn't always have to be a notepad, the main thing is to hold on to the energy of the idea. *P.J. Pereira: »Sometimes it happens when I'm almost sleeping. I have got an idea and I say okay I am going to do that tomorrow and I can't sleep*

until I get up, turn the computer on and send myself an email to the office, and when I have sent that I can sleep.«

How well prepared are you to record unexpected ideas immediately?

Force Yourself to Another Idea

Ideas can happen in a relaxed state of mind or under extreme pressure. In order to find an antipode to tension, Top-Creatives invent their own games to put themselves under pressure or to overcome exhaustion. *Donna Weinheim: »I like to play a little game with myself, that last idea before I go home thing. It's just a matter of playing games with yourself. If I come up with one more idea, I can go home.«*

It's rather like exercise, the more you exercise, the more energy you have to exercise.

Mike Wells

This playfulness becomes more important than the task. The intention is not really to get an additional idea, but rather to develop an idea based on playful conditions. This is also a good training to find more and better ideas. *Mike Wells: »It's rather like exercise, the more you exercise, the more energy you have to exercise. Often if you're tired, the way to get more energy is to exercise. So you then feel invigorated so you've got more energy. Expanding energy creates energy. Resting does not create energy.«*

As it gets later at night, the rational resistance to "silly ideas" is reduced. So that ideas can show up, while at other times of the day most logical thoughts would have fought against them. *Sean Nassy: »It tends to come in when I am totally tired and burned and frustrated.«*

Paul Spencer: »*I couldn't have come up with it if I hadn't been pushed. I was thinking 'We're not gonna come up with any more commercials' and I came up with the best commercial I've ever done.*«

This kind of relaxation can be brought about with a small trick. *Paul Spencer:* »*If I'm really tense, I can't perform at all. I learnt in voice-overs or with actors to tell them, 'okay we already have it, don't worry, we already have a perfect version, but let's do another one'. And then all the pressure is off so they can really do it.*«

> What playful approach could force yourself
> to have another good idea?

Play with Last-Minute Deadlines

Deadlines can make you tense, but can also relax you. That's why for some Top-Creatives deadlines are seen as helpful in getting them to concentrate on the task. Some of them even use deadlines as a method. They let things lie until the last day. *Hernan Ponce:* »*Finally, on last day when you have to present it, something appears. It's magical. It's pressure, high pressure.*«

Deadlines can frighten you, and this can also increase your concentration. *Bob Isherwood:* »*I always work on a fear factor, I notice I quite often leave a thing to the last minute so I am totally adrenaline pumped and very focussed.*« Deadlines make the focus to an assignment more intense and they may produce a higher degree of motivation.

Finally, on last day when you have to present it, something appears. It's magical. It's pressure, high pressure.

Hernan Ponce

Many Top-Creatives also use time pressure to tame their perfectionism. *David Caballero: »Sometimes I think, thank God we've got timings and schedules and deadlines to meet because if we didn't, all work would take me a year or so.«*

How much time-pressure do you need to work with concentration?

It is Important, but it's Only Advertising

Not taking your own work too seriously relaxes you. And if you're not able to joke about your work, you'll find it very difficult to create something entertaining for others.

Gerard Stamp: »Advertising should entertain, it's got to add something to people's lives rather than abuse people. It's our duty to entertain, to add, not to use that just to shout at people.«

A high work standard will make advertising valuable, so it gives people and their perception of the world a special meaning. But it's the playing with this meaning and our senses, that lets Great Ideas work far beyond the advertising world.

*I can't take advertising that seriously.
I have to be relaxed
in getting into the ideas.*

Rob Kitchen

Rob Kitchen: »*I can't take advertising that seriously. I have to be relaxed in getting into the ideas. So taking the piss, or being irreverent or being flippant, is really important. Even the serious advertising should have fun doing it.*«

So not taking advertising too seriously can be stimulating and relaxing.

What would make you have more fun in your job?

☆

How to Work with an Idea without Losing It:

You
can't lose

In order to describe an idea you need words and images. If you use too many, the idea will quickly become too heavy, if you use too few, the idea will be unclear and open and the spark can't fly over. The real art is to use just enough material to create an exciting framework, so that the idea can be understood and that the observer can fill it with his own imagination. If you don't manage this you will lose a headline or image, but not an idea.

an idea

Javi Carro

The Description of an Idea Gives Access
to the Energy of an Idea

Many Creatives have Great Ideas but often they can't describe them in a way that others will understand their enthusiasm for the idea. This is usually because they have not chosen the right "material", the right words, images, sounds. The most important thing when describing an idea is therefore, that the idea is the focus point and not the form it's presented in.

Alexandra Taylor: »*I'm keeping true to the idea all the time. You mustn't let the art direction get in the way of the idea.*«

Art Direction is the art of giving an idea "Direction". This direction giving should always be there to serve the idea, not the other way around. At this point the execution does not have a function of its own. Otherwise it is not a direction but "art pour l'art". Also using a computer too early on can lead to a fixed manifestation too soon, without the idea being in its best form. Barbara Schmidt: »*Young talents often interchange form and idea.*«

First work out a brilliant concept,
then play with the design of it.

Top-Creatives differentiate between the idea and their handicraft that they use as a Copywriter or Art Director. They look for a strong concept of the idea, which will direct them during materialisation. Alexandra Taylor: »*The concept is the most important thing. It doesn't matter how much you play around with the design of it, if the concept of the initial idea is not strong, then forget it. I'll only art direct great ads.*«

Donna Weinheim: »*If it doesn't start out with a good idea, it's never good.*« In order to develop the first tender perception of an idea and channel the energy of the idea towards its goal, Top-Creatives prefer to work with visual, audio and sensitive tools. The visual representation of an idea can be seen as the main thing. Creatives project vivid images in the air, already partly arranged, multi-coloured, as big movie screens or like on a TV screen.

Hernan Ponce: »*I have a visual up here, like a balloon, it's a thinking balloon. I watch it and say that's good. It may then be really different to what I had imagined.*« These and other image processing methods describe the ability to project energy in the form of images from inside to outside.

So the perception and expression of ideas by Top-Creatives goes a lot further than the well-known request to just describe the idea to someone else on the telephone. They use a combination of skills that allows for a virtuous interaction with the idea, before it has not yet been channelled into its final best form. The energy of the idea in this phase still escapes easily, so it has to be kept safe, so that nothing of it gets lost.

For this purpose, it's very important to clearly differentiate between the various levels of an idea. The differentiation between the Strategic Proposition (Benefit Idea), the Higher Concept (Lead Idea) and the Execution Idea (handcrafted by visuals, words or sounds) are absolutely necessary for the safe variation and the energy management of the idea.

Nick Worthington: »*You do get a straight idea in your head and it takes a bit of articulation to get it out of your head, and to work out what it is you have seen or just thought.*« The decision as to how much material is needed and how much you can do without, is also important to be able to bring out the idea in all its strength. But this can also be learned: *Nick Worthington* on himself and his partner John Gorse: »*We weren't very good when we started. We weren't naturals. We probably had a lot of good ideas, but we had no real idea about this sort of discipline, or how to put them down. What elements you need and what you don't need. We'd put too much in, or not enough.*«

Often an idea is only a small seed, which can be helped to grow with targeted interventions – similar to a good meal where the decisive ingredients are added by and by, to give it that extra kick, the perfect seasoning. *Xavi Garcias:* »*The idea is that you use a lot of ingredients and then suddenly the dish takes shape, but the question is not this last ingredient but the sum of them all,*

all the inputs you received are important. The order is quite random, and the last ingredient can come anywhere. The important thing is that when you start doing a campaign, you don't stop receiving inputs.«

In order to determine if your Description of an Idea already meets these requirements, you can ask yourself:

☆ Have you chosen the right words and images to make the great energy of the idea visible to others?

☆ Can you reduce the idea to one sentence or a key visual so that the energy is kept in its essence?

☆ Can you see the idea from different angles so you can recognize its strengths, and in particular, its weaknesses?

☆ Can you clearly differentiate the lead idea and higher concept from the benefit and the execution of the Idea?

☆ Have you got sufficient distance from the idea so that you keep an open mind for all improvements anybody gives?

If you can answer these questions with "yes", you will be able to hold the energy of an idea elegantly with playful effortlessness, to develop it, reject it or improve it. In particular you will be able to describe it in a form that not only excites yourself but also excites others. If not, you are perhaps caught in the energy of the idea and will more likely become obsessed with it. So you are being managed by the idea instead of the other way around. You are looking at your idea from one side only and overlooking the great chance, which a radical or minimal change of the idea has to offer. In this case, you only know good or bad ideas and will find it very difficult to steer the inspirational power of your ideas. The following tips will help you to build a better basis to describe your ideas.

Develop a Precise Personal Vision of the Idea

The more people you bring into contact with your idea, the more secure your vision of the idea should be. In order to strengthen and develop this, Top-Creatives visualise the idea very precisely. They play several possibilities through in their own "personal head movie". *Hansjörg Zürcher:* »*I try to develop the film in my head so that I can actually say exactly what the finished film will look like. It's like a picture screen.*«

The imagination is like an editing machine with thousands of images and you can play with them.

Xavi Garcias

With their imagination, Top-Creatives achieve a very high speed in exchanging images in their heads. This skill is not just limited to the visual process but also includes feeling and hearing possible soundtracks or voiceovers. *Xavi Garcias:* »*The imagination is like an editing machine with thousands of images and you can play with them. I have visuals, cinemascope. Huge. Huge in colour. If you want you can smell a flower without smelling a flower.*«

This definite perception increases the ideas safety when it's being executed. Because Top-Creatives have already seen it before, they know exactly what they want when it comes to production. *Dave Linne:* »*I always see the spot in my head. You tend to see exactly how the commercial will be shot. What the actors are doing, I see the whole thing in my head. How I imagined it being. Perfectly edited. There are other spots, other ideas you come up with where you come to a fork in the road and you know it goes good or bad. You know it's going to be good because you can see it all happening.*«

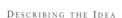

It's very seldom that they actually manage to get the exact shape and performance that they had envisioned with their inner eye. *Xavi Garcias: »Perhaps there's a few that surprised me at the end, but normally the imagination is richer than what one can physically produce.«*

How can you generate an even more vivid vision of your idea?

Exaggerate the Logic into the Unexpected

Similar to jokes, if you want to break through perception limits, "expanding the logic" can lead to a new surprise and to a new idea quality. *John Hunt: »The logic normally gets you half way and then you start going laterally. So after the first step you start taking that logic and stretching it so that it's still relevant, but it's a little unexpected.«* In order to get dog food, lots of dogs will jump up high. In the commercial "Sharky" this logic is exaggerated and a dog jumps, completely illogically, several floors high.

John Hunt: »The team kept trying to find expressions of how a dog would show his desire. Jumping up 50 to 60 feet, Sharky is very relevant but unexpected.«

You should not let yourself be satisfied too early with a "correct logical" idea, but rather play around with it as long as it's still soft and flexible. This is what happened with the "Ape"-Commercial from HBO, where originally a parrot was supposed to quote classic film lines instead of the ape. *Don Schneider: »It was a concept of someone or something who's been exposed to HBO and would know all these classic lines from the movies. That spot was born, but it actually started with a parrot.«*

Another example is the Pepsi commercial "Apartment 10G" which originally describes the story of a guy who goes off to get a Pepsi for a girl, and goes down a couple of floors to get it, knocks on a window, and then returns with the Pepsi. In this case, Michael Patti and Don Schneider added in quite a lot of things and expanded the idea. In the new version the hero, this time it's Michael J. Fox, has to run from a fire, overcome a traffic jam, escape from an angry dog into a car until he finally ends up at the Pepsi dispenser, which is blocked by a motor cycle gang. The question that led to this exaggeration according to *Michael Patti* was: »**How much stuff can you throw in his way and he still goes to get the Diet Pepsi for the girl and for himself. So it just sort of grew and grew and grew.**«

The logic normally gets you half way and then you start going laterally.

John Hunt

This method of working is a good alternative to the usual rejection of ideas, because it takes what was once an unspectacular idea and puts it into a new form, and as a result, on a new energy level. Interestingly enough in this idea, Michael J. Fox is not the focus point, the story is, which would also have worked without him. In general, Top-Creatives only use stars for an unusual execution and not as a substitute for an idea.

How can you bring the logic that is the basis of your idea to the boiling point?

110 Reduce the Idea to a Key Visual

In order to further reduce and consolidate the idea, it should be reduced to a key visual, which contains all the important "essences". This will identify and exclude unnecessary weight. *Gianfranco Marabelli:* »**The idea started with a poster, and sometimes I notice that when an idea comes from an image, a key frame idea, the poster idea is better because you are really**

sure that there is a key frame. When you can describe a commercial in a poster, often it is a good commercial because the audience have in mind a key frame.«

Mike Wells: »You've to get rid of everything which is distracting and home it right down to the most simple image you can think of.«

In the case of strong and reduced ideas, even complex TV scripts can be transferred to other media. *Hernan Ponce: »It is a good idea when you can put the idea of a TV commercial into an outdoor poster.«* In the end, a TV or cinema-spot consists of over 20 images per second; at 30 seconds and over 600 images there should be at least one that expresses the core idea.

Consolidating the idea into one single image also allows freedom for new interpretation possibilities. For Don Schneider and Michael Patti the key visual functions as a sort of stenography. *Michael Patti: »He can draw one visual and you can see the whole spot in there. We don't have to draw the frame by frame thing because we talk it out so much.«*

You've to get rid of everything which is distracting and home it right down to the most simple image you can think of.

Mike Wells

With this method, the danger of distraction through loss of energy and unfocussed ideas is reduced. It is basically the art of translating a benefit into a visual concept. And as a result, to profit from the clarity and speed of a strong visual language. Because this kind of visual concept is strongly reduced, many good TV-ideas even work without a voice-over. *Donna Weinheim: »People sometimes turn the sound down, so for me that's even more lucky because the strength of the commercial just rests on what the pictures start out being, what it's communicating.«*

To what key-visual could you reduce the idea?

Reduce the Idea to its Essence

It is usually words and images that let us experience an idea, that let us tell the story. In this way every image and every word is an execution. One good way of testing whether this execution will also produce a good idea is to reduce the idea to its essence. *Erik Voser:* »*I believe that you can improve advertising by reducing the idea. So much so that after the reduction only the essence of the idea remains.*«

You can distil the essence of a message until you can't take anything away anymore. Sometimes, however, it can happen that there is nothing left. This is an indication that the idea was not strong enough and was just a combination of different execution ideas.

I believe that you can improve advertising by reducing the idea. So much so that after the reduction only the essence of the idea remains.

Erik Voser

Therefore, Top-Creatives work deeply into the material to arrive at an essence and use energy that is authentic and true. *Susan Hoffman:* »*I always try and get down to the core, instead of 'I saw this cool technique, I want to use it'. I always try and go back to what is the heart and soul of this brand, or what is the heart and soul of this idea, as opposed to what is a cool way to do a commercial.*«

The respective heart of the Nike brand was described as follows. *Susan Hoffman:* »*It's 'authentic sports'. It can be served up in different ways, it can be humour, it can be serious, but in the end it needs to feel it's authentic to sport.*« You can feel this energy in every single piece of communication for Nike.

What is the real heart of the idea that you want to bring to life?

Produce the Idea Completely in Your Head

You will become very quick if you produce the idea completely in your head. *Marcello Serpa:* »*I cut my layouts out in my head, before they get to paper. It's like having a stencil with a double page. At that moment when the image appears, I know exactly how I am going to do it. Then it doesn't take long until I actually do it.*«

In this case, it can be either a screen, a newspaper or a TV format. The movements are usually not harmonious but rather jump from one image to another. *Mike Wells:* »*There are very big colourful pictures, full-screen. You just change it inside your head. Just move it around, change the colours, it's a bit like dreaming.*«

This is also true for the headline-integration in print motives. *Matthias Freuler:* »*I always cut out the headline in my head. It is in my head but I project it then on to the respective page and I can see the finished ad. I can also see how the headline is going to look, it looks different in the end of course, but I need to have a finished picture in my head so that I can imagine it.*«

This exact image of the idea can also provide an in-detail feeling for the evaluation of the work carried out later.

How many different "Head-Layouts" can you produce for your idea?

Train your "Inner 3D-Films"

Top-Creatives have developed the skill of imagining, changing and of course, improving complete TV-Spots in their heads. *Donna Weinheim:* »*You see it from beginning to end. You see it moving, you play it, I guess, if you do enough commercials, it's like anything else, you train yourself to see it moving through your head.*«

The person's head then becomes a pre-production place. *Xavi Garcias: »Of course, you can change the picture. Furthermore, you can change it at tremendous speed. Nothing is as fast as the mind.«*

Nothing is as fast as the mind.

Xavi Garcias

In order to develop the feeling, aesthetics and dramaturgy of a commercial it is important to be able to visually imagine all of the dimensions. *Xavi Garcias: »It's not a picture, it's 3D. I see it all done real finished, on TV, in the newspaper as if you had already seen it before. All the prior work was abstract. But the idea I see real in detail.«*

How can you receive an even clearer, multi-dimensional impression of the idea?

Work with a Pencil and not with the Computer

When we work with the energy of ideas, that show up quickly, we need fast tools so that we can process them. But the minute we turn on a computer we are automatically caught up with the execution of the idea and we slow down. We are busy with the layout, text, typo and colour, instead of with the idea. We lose valuable time here, at least as long as the description of the idea is not finished. Most Top-Creatives therefore work with a pencil and a simple sheet of paper.

Toni Segarra: »I work with ballpen on the paper, not with computers, and I try to draw the visuals that come to my mind. Usually they are just of positions or strong visuals, but simple visuals.«

By drawing with the pencil, we give our thoughts more expression and reduce the idea to the essentials, to simplicity. Ideas usually become complicated on their own. Using simple tools support the simplicity of Great Ideas.

How can you bring the idea into an even simpler more reduced form?

Talk to Your Idea

Many Top-Creatives carry on a dialogue with their work so that they can gain additional information to improve the idea at hand.

Dan Wieden: »To me there's always a sense of you are not creating something, you're in a dialogue with the work itself and you need to listen to the work and respond to what it is saying. You can't be pushing it all the time, because then you delude yourself, you need to somehow have this conversation. You are communicating with something and pulling it up out of nonexistence into existence. But it will resist at times and it will give you things at times.«

Ask the idea what it is lacking, what could be changed? What works incorrectly or is clumsy? What is still over the top? What is not harmonious or appears untrue? What has not got to the point yet?

Edwin Veelo: »For me, it has got to speak to me. I'm very quick in seeing when it's trying to say something and it isn't.«

What exciting questions can you ask your idea?

Develop the Idea from the Sound of the Product

Because we also recognize truth in the sound of someone's voice, the development of a "voice" for the product or an idea is a perfectly natural process for Top-Creatives.

I can do up to about 100 layouts, playing around

Alexandra Taylor

with it and approving it and moving on and on and on.

Steve Simpson: »We came up with a look and a tone of voice that was at least recognisably consistent and quite clearly different from what the competitors were doing.«

This tone can also be in a picture or a layout. *Alexandra Taylor: »I put the ad down on the floor and thought about the tone, do I want this to be quite soft and quiet, or do I want it to be loud and very confident? I can do up to about 100 layouts, playing around with it and approving it and moving on and on and on.«*

In what language, in what tone, would the idea develop the most strength?

Tell the Idea as a Good Story

When Top-Creatives develop their stories, dialogues and characters it is very important for them that they sound real. The first possibility to check this out is with ourselves. *Jon Moore: »I tend to tell stories, I'm telling myself stories over and over again, 'til a story clicks', until it feels right, so you play around with the different elements. I don't connect A to B. I'm telling some kind of a*

story and just how that story comes out and how that story makes sense with the product and makes sense with the point of the product.«

This story must be authentic and formed by human awareness, these are the factors that make the story believable. *Jon Moore:* »*Just sitting there until you really have it and going through the dialogue until it really rings true. I think that people can relate to that ... I know that guy, I know that person, there's somebody down my block just like that.«*

So make sure that you develop stories with the right main characters, so that the energy, the truth and the authenticity will give your ideas strength.

With what story or metaphor could you even better transport your message?

Check whether Your Idea is Easy for Others to Understand

With every good idea, many others will try to come to life too, we have to reject those, so that the chosen idea is clear and understandable, in its form and structure. *Xavi Garcias:* »*Advertising is a permanent rejection of things. It's not adding things, it's rejecting things.«*

Michael Volkmer: »*If you have to explain how it works something is wrong.«*

Advertising is a permanent rejection of things. It's not adding things, it's rejecting things.

Xavi Garcias

This is true, regardless in which medium the idea is to be used. *Bob Isherwood:* »*I think that is the key element of a good idea, it is simplicity and it's obviousness executed in a way that no one has imagined.*«

Jeff Goodby: »*To make an idea sharper, you really have to do two things, you really have to decide what the parts of it are you want to make sharp, and then you have to decide what parts are really not relevant to what you are trying to accomplish, and throw those parts away.*«

What could you leave out to make the idea more understandable?

Make the First Second Exciting

A well-known advertising expression says: people don't look at advertising but at what interests them. If there is something unknown and surprising in the advertisement it will usually grab our attention immediately, so we want to see more. *Donna Weinheim:* »*I have one rule I don't always follow, that if in the first five seconds your picture looks like something that no one has ever seen before, it's interesting. I think the first five seconds are critical to getting someone's attention.*«

Attention is mostly caught when we vary from the norm. This is valid not only for TV, but also for ideas in other media. *Gerard Stamp:* »*Thinking hard about how to make this ad as different as you can from anything that's run before.*«

I think the first five seconds are critical
to getting someone's attention.
Donna Weinheim

Donna Weinheim: »*Coming up with ideas really means coming up with things that no one has thought before, and that's always hard because it's unchartered territory, so it's unchartered thinking. You start out really in an abstract world and the beauty is, there are no rules. If there were rules then there wouldn't be unchartered territory.*«

What would be an even more exciting
first impression for your idea?

Find an Unexpected Twist

A surprise is always made up of two parts. The part that we expect and the part we don't expect. Most advertising is full of examples where we already know the script. An "unexpected twist" can therefore only happen if we believe that we already know what is going to happen.

Lee Garfinkel: »*I'm always looking for the twist, I used to do stand-up comedy, I was writing before I got into advertising and I was performing. I wasn't that good at it but you learn what's funny and what's not, and one of the basics of comedy is surprise.*«

With the demand to do exactly the opposite, we can find such new perspectives and systematically move from the norm through the contradiction to the abnormal. *Xavi Garcias:* »*I like to think of images that contradict what you want to really say.* «

What would be the opposite from
what you want to say?

Let the Viewers Take Part in the Idea

Sometimes the ideas are perfected into the tiniest detail and everything is finished and arranged. The observer however, only makes the actual connection with the idea, when there is enough room to find something personally interesting in it. *Jeff Goodby: »Bad advertising, like bad art and bad anything, provides all the clues and just kind of throws it all at you and expects that some of it is going to stick to your brain somehow.«*

Top-Creatives consciously look for a kind of gap that the observer can fill with his own feelings and fantasies. This means they don't define everything beforehand, but rather let the observer have some fun, completing the message for himself. The method is comparable to kids painting by numbers.

Rich Silverstein: »What I really like to do is have people think, to challenge people. We put the dots out there and you connect the dots. You participate in the advertising, that what's we like to do.« In this way the observer is actively involved in the work and has a far more intensive connection to the idea.

*How could you get the observer more involved
in the interpretation of the idea?*

Keep the Idea Open for Your Partner

Even if Top-Creatives initially find their own standpoint from where they develop the idea, it is very important to them to give their partners the chance to improve the idea with additional thoughts and new aspects. For this reason, they keep the idea open and do not manifest it too tightly. *Michael Patti: »I scribble it down but leave it fresh, and don't try to work on it totally by myself. I think that's the healthiest environment for when an idea is new. Don (Schneider) adds something that I don't expect and that gets me excited, and vice versa.«*

The exchange and the sharing of this "Seed of an Idea" also keeps the material safer that you will be working on later. *Nick Worthington:* **»We produce maybe 50 to 100 ideas and unless one really jumps out through the process, then I give John all mine and he gives me all his, and I'll just go through all him and I'll pick out the ones that jump out to me and he'll do the same with mine and we'll get a sort of a pool of ideas. Quite often we'll come up with the same idea or an idea that is very similar, and that's always a sign that if we both like it, then it's interesting.«**

Quite often we'll come up with the same idea or an idea that is very similar, and that's always a sign that if we both like it, then it's interesting.

Nick Worthington

Mutual inspiration is dependent on a mutual exchange of information. The exchange of idea fragments gives both partners the possibility to play with the other's idea and increases security in the evaluation of the idea. *Bob Moore:* **»Generally, when an idea is really good, we are both very excited about it, I'll write something and he will say 'Wow, this is great, let me try and play with it for a couple of days', or 'that's not so great, maybe try writing it like this' and the same goes for the art direction.«**

How can you pick up the core of your partner's idea more openly?

Inspire Yourself and Others with Exciting Aspects

A positive mental attitude is not only relaxing for yourself and others, it also generates a positive curiosity, and as such, a direction oriented attention onto the problem and the product.

Rich Silverstein: »**I get really excited about every project, I get them excited. Every time we start a project creative people are very cynical and it's like 'who cares about that product', 'who drinks milk', 'who wants another cruise line', that's what they say every time. What you have to do is break that, you have to get them excited, so I wave the flag.**«

Generating positive attention towards the product or the assignment puts your entire organism into a state of curious tension. This is inspiring for you and others. In particular, if the product seems to be boring or the market appears to be over-saturated.

What additional exciting aspects can you get out of the assignment or the product?

Always have a Positive Approach to Work

Cynicism, sarcasm or bad jokes are like bad ideas. They block and withdraw energy instead of focussing it. They are toxic for ideas. A positive atmosphere and constructive criticism make it easier to perceive what is good about an idea. *Wells Packard:* »**You have to get it to that level where you can get other people excited about it. To be motivated about that project you must have a certain amount of passion or personal commitment to it.**«

There's a rule, you have to be positive.

Don Schneider

In particular, as long as an idea is only the seed of an idea, a positive overall attitude helps to keep it alive, instead of destroying it.

195

Don Schneider: »There's a rule, you have to be positive. What you have to do is either top it, add to it or change it, and if you don't like to change it to something better, add something positive. Otherwise when your partner says it stinks, you sit like this for the next hour, playing with pencils, it brings in this negativity so you have to stay positive.«

In particular the rejection of ideas should take place decisively, understandably, and with a basic positive attitude, otherwise it can lead to a negative atmosphere. *Rich Silverstein: »The biggest killer of ideas is saying no. Just negative, like nah, that's not good, if you keep saying that you just get in a negative mood.«*

How can you make your working atmosphere more positive?

Look for the Big Spark, even in a Bad Execution

The idea is not always transformed into words or pictures in its optimal form. One skill that separates Top-Creatives from others, is to be able to see the good in bad ideas, and as a result, to keep such ideas alive, that otherwise would have been thrown out because of their bad execution.

Sometimes the idea is camouflaged, ideas play hide and seek. You can only see a little bit but the rest is revealed.

Enrico Bonomini

Ted Sann: »It takes you about thirty seconds to read it and there's no idea, there's nothing in it and you say okay, next. And there is one that's okay, that's smart, that's got the beginning of the good idea, let's talk about that.«

Processing chances and seeing possibilities that others don't see, plays a big role in discovering the seed of an idea and to keeping it alive – especially for a Creative Director. *Enrico Bonomini:* »*When you listen to other people's ideas you have got to be able to keep listening and pick out the one little spark perhaps from the great chaos of everything. Sometimes the idea is camouflaged, ideas play hide and seek. You can only see a little bit but the rest is revealed.*«

Often you will find good ideas in bad executions. Active and positive listening is therefore a very important skill. *Jeff Goodby:* »*I'm good at listening to other people's ideas and figuring out with them what they can do with them, to make them better, to fix them, to make them more relevant. But also help them handle the pain of throwing them away.*«

What seed from the existing idea could you bring into a far better form?

How to Judge an Idea Professionally:

If it's fine
it doesn't happen,

The evaluation of an idea is the most critical step in the Creative Process. A positive evaluation ends the search for even better ideas. Only a negative evaluation of the idea keeps the Creative Process going. So the Idea Evaluation steers the Finding of the Idea Process. High standards and the extremely tough evaluation of the idea ensures that Top-Creatives spend more time than others looking for better ideas. That's why they find them.

if it's great,

it happens

Rich Silverstein

The Evaluation of the Idea must Work as a Quality Control without Compromises

The evaluation of the idea interrupts the Find the Idea Process or keeps it going. It steers the Creative Process far more than Finding the Idea does. That is why all creative award shows are "Idea Evaluation Competitions" where an external institution judges the quality of the idea. Find the Idea brings the idea to life. A tough idea evaluation makes it strong, or kills it, because it checks if the idea really has great quality. That is why you could also say:

Top-Creatives are much more Top-Creative Judges setting highest standards.

Only if you reject good ideas you will have a chance to move on to a Great Idea. That is why the criteria that is used by Top-Creatives as the basis for the evaluation is so tough. This is the only way to avoid having bad or average ideas continued or even produced. Strangely enough, the good ideas are far more dangerous than the bad ones because they will not be rejected so easily and may just mess up the chance of a very good idea. *Nick Worthington: »It's that area of good work which everyone gets lost in. Some people say they think it's fantastic and some people say they think it's terrible, but genuinely really, really good stuff everybody agrees it is good.«*

The fact that an idea is sold does not mean that it is good, but rather that it was paid for.

Loz Simpson: »Look at the crap you see, somebody let it through. A Creative Director in the agency said yes, I'll sign that, take it down to the client, and then the client bought it.«

The standard requirements placed on the work determine its level. In an advertising agency the Creative Director defines this. He is not primarily there to get ideas. His function is more to reject good ideas. The more he is able to do this, the better the chance will be that very good ideas are generated. *Nick Worthington: »When we were at BBH, I would say 70 or 80 per cent of the work we did never got out of the door.«*

While Top-Creatives are very relaxed in Finding an Idea and very tough in the evaluation phase, the average Creative Process usually runs the other way around: The "usual" Creative searches for new ideas very tensed up, instead being of relaxed and enjoying it, and then later he is too exhausted and laid-back to evaluate the idea. That also explains why there are so many mediocre ideas out there that were released by responsible decision makers. They simply agreed on a somewhat low level, when evaluating, selling or buying the idea.

If you want to improve your criteria you can basically judge every idea according to two parameters. First, "is the idea rationally right, is it on strategy", and secondly "is the idea surprising and new?" A good idea will score points on both counts. *Loz Simpson: »When you are young you come up with crazy ideas and you think it's a crazy idea, it must be good. After you have learned you realize that the crazy idea has to have one foot in that world, it has to be relevant, it has to be right. It is judgement, your judgement develops. You have seen more, you have made mistakes, you have learned.«*

The Creative Brief offers the best basis on which to check if What the idea expresses is right. *Dave Linne: »The biggest thing that'd kill an idea, is being off strategy. Be mad about yourself if something dies because of being off strategy.«*

*The direction of the energy determines
if an idea is right or wrong.*

The strategy should allow for answers to the following questions: Does the idea solve the problem in a relevant and believable manner? Is it simple enough to be easily understood? Is the idea based on unique information, in order to differentiate the product effectively in its market? Is it connected to the product, and does it place the product or the brand in the centre? Does the idea have the right kind of tone, and is it seen as suitable for the brand and strengthens it?

Whether an idea is right can largely be judged according to rational, objective criteria. *Alexandra Taylor: »When I have to approve work I think does that answer the proposition about this product, about this brand? Does it answer the client's problem, and is it great art? If it answers those two boxes for me then it's good enough.«*

Whereas, the examination of whether an idea is right and "on strategy" can be done objectively, the judgement of the originality is far more subjective. Here, it helps to evaluate the idea on its energy.

The lasting intensity of the perceived energy determines the originality of the idea.

Great Ideas can be identified by their energetic magnetic power, which you can feel physically. This includes the drive with which you want to implement the idea, or perhaps the fear that somebody will get there before you, because the solution is sometimes so obvious. The physical experience of these impulses differentiates between the energy of a Great Idea and a normal idea. For many Top-Creatives, a further distinction of this energy, is the risk with which a really new idea is associated. Will the client buy it? Can you produce it like this? Will it still be as brilliant after the production as we imagined it would be? Will it work? *Susan Hoffman: »I think people always should be scared of their advertising a little because if it is not unusual, then it's not going to open up the consumer's eyes.«*

Bob Moore: »You go 'WOW, that's scary work', or 'that's really exciting', or 'that's brutally honest'. You get the feeling when it's like something you haven't seen before, or your interpretation of something that you've seen before but in entirely new way.«

For this reason, unusual campaign ideas are closely connected with the business courage of the management and company personalities, who are often as well known as the company itself. That is why:

Someone who does not want to carry responsibility for new things should not be responsible for deciding on ideas.

A client who has no courage to carry the risk of a new idea, will most likely see advertising as safely holding on to present standards, more than as an investment in the future, and will probably go for usual and supposedly certain solutions, and may rely more on others and market research than on himself. *Dan Wieden: »Worrying too much about what other people will think, is the biggest problem. That's where things become too user-friendly. You need to create things that are personally powerful to you. If they are powerful to you, they will be powerful to other people, maybe not everybody but enough people.«*

Before you test an idea until everybody likes it, reject it and develop a new idea that you can stand up for and that is strong enough.

Xavi Garcias: »Sooner or later, the worst thing that can happen is that you conform, or try to bring life to something that is dead.«

Checking whether an idea is on strategy or not, is relatively easy when based on rational criteria and a precise strategy. It is much more difficult and more subjective to evaluate whether the idea has enough energy, enough potential. You will be able to estimate this more effectively by using the following criteria:

- ☆ Do you feel the inspiration power of the idea leading you to many other ideas, that usually come flowingly after the idea?
- ☆ Can you feel the drive of the idea, and do you urgently want to see it, produce it and bring it to life?
- ☆ Can you feel the risk of the idea, and does this motivate you because it shows you something completely new?
- ☆ Do you feel pride in the idea and would just love to show or tell everybody about it?

☆ Do you still feel the power and truth that is going to keep exciting you and others the next day when you have a little distance from the idea?

If you can answer these questions with "yes", you really do have a powerful idea, the energy of which will inspire many other people. If not however, you will be uncertain and instead you will be post-rationalising the idea. You will be arguing that the idea is right but your heart won't really be in it. Most of all, you will not be excited about it. The following tips and questions will definitely make your idea evaluation more certain, and increase its standards.

Evaluate the Idea Honestly, Regardless of Who it Comes from

All Top-Creatives have always emphasised the importance of an honest and un-political evaluation of the work. For that reason it is very helpful if the creative work in the company has the highest priority, so that neither the client, employees or your own ego get in the way.

Rich Silverstein: »**When they're getting the judgment from me, it's very honest – there's no game that I'm playing – there's no politics. A person in the mail room could have a better idea than me and it would be okay and that's what we try to do here.**«

Rich Silverstein

Because the evaluation is directed at making no compromises on the quality of the work, a tougher evaluation can be more easily digested and helps you to learn. *Alexandra Taylor:* »**I'm known to be direct but you have to, they want the truth, they want to know how they can improve on it.**«

A tough and open evaluation, whoever it comes from, is for many Top-Creatives the basis on which trust can be built. *Gerard Stamp:* »**I've got to be honest about what I like, what I dislike, and integrity is, again, pretty close, it's not lying to people, not using people, getting people to trust me.**«

Are you always 100 per cent honest to yourself and others when evaluating the ideas?

Sharpen up Your Evaluation Criteria

An idea that has been approved of once, will inevitably take its course in the execution, presentation and later in production. As the idea continues to materialise, it will become more firm, slower, and more expensive. It will take more time and energy from others. To make sure that this energy is invested effectively in the best idea, applying highest standards in the search for the idea and its evaluation, is extremely important.

If I say it's okay that means go back and do it again because most advertising is okay.

Lee Garfinkel

Ted Sann: »*You have to be hyper critical because you can really talk yourself into liking things because you are sitting there working and you've got a deadline and you've got clients screaming for work and it's very easy to get satisfied collectively and you say okay we got it. You really have to be ready to throw it out and start over again. If you're too easily satisfied with everything you're going to be in big trouble.*«

This makes it clear why Top-Creatives actually place highest demands on their own and other peoples' work. Because in the long run you can only change the output of a Creative System by intensifying and raising the evaluation criteria. *Rich Silverstein: »We set the standard so high, I just don't say 'Oh that's fine', if it's 'fine' it doesn't happen, if it's great, it happens.«*

Lee Garfinkel: »I used to have a sign up on my wall: If I say it's okay that means go back and do it again because most advertising is okay. Someone had a line that 'good is the enemy of great', which I agree because if you've a tendency to say it's good people will stop working.«

With what additional demands can you increase your own personal standards?

Check whether the Idea Really Excites You

In order to evaluate if an idea is good we usually ask ourselves: Is it right? Does it communicate a, b, c, d ,e? In the excitement of having answered everything with "yes", we often forget to ask the really important question: Am I emotionally touched? If we apply the first method and we can tick off the components a, b, etc., in the end we will only have a "correct communication". The emotional and gut feeling is left behind. For this reason, Top-Creatives first check whether the idea touches and inspires people. *P.J. Pereira: »I begin from the heart, not the mind. The heart is much easier to talk to.«*

It's satisfaction, somewhere between the stomach and the brain and the guts.

Felix de Castro

Chuck Carlson: »It has got to put a spark in me. It's got to be fresh and creative and really gets your blood flowing. Go through all these checklists to make sure it is really right for the situation but the first thing is, it puts a smile on your face.«

What is the benefit of communication that hits the mark, but is not exciting? A communication idea that is right, but does not surprise anybody, simply does not make the most out of the clients budget. *Felix de Castro: »I recognize it is brilliant, because it makes me laugh, because I think it's original and outstanding. It's a feeling, rather than something rational. It's satisfaction, somewhere between the stomach and the brain and the guts.«*

Rich Silverstein: »They came into my room and they said: we have got this idea, 'see what develops' (for Polaroid) and I went 'that's it'. I meant, it was like instant to me. When I hear it and it feels right it's going to be right and that one felt right.«

Do you feel the energy of the idea immediately and also physically?

Use Your Dissatisfaction to Drive Yourself to High-Performance

Top-Creatives are highly self-motivated to constant high-performance. They are never really satisfied with what they have done. Even when their work has already received several awards. Constant dissatisfaction is the key to ever increasing standards. This is how Top-Creatives bring themselves to new borders, over and over again.

Dan Wieden: »The minute you are finished with something, you are dissatisfied with it almost instinctively. That's what drives you on to the next thing.«

This is how Top-Creatives get the most out of themselves. *Jon Matthews:* »***There are a million ways to do stuff and there is probably one better than the one you have done.***«

Positive dissatisfaction generates new energy that can be used to improve ideas. *Xavi Garcias:* »***I never feel 100 per cent happy with what I've done.***«

*How can you make better use of your own dissatisfaction
or that of your team?*

Trust Your Physical Reaction

When Top-Creatives receive the idea, or see somebody else's idea for the first time, they rely on their physical reaction. This shows you quickly and uncensored if an idea is good or not. *Barbara Schmidt:* »***When you get goose bumps and you notice the reaction in yourself and no longer have doubts.***«

That's about feel with your heart, listen to your heart.

John Hegarty

Milka Pogliani: »***When you feel something right or wrong, normally your body reacts to things in a proper way, it's not your mind, with your mind you have got a lot of schemes, a lot of different issues and I think stereotype reactions as well.***«

Such awareness can be felt in very varying sensual ways. *Milka Pogliani:* »***When you have a good idea you can recognize it, you smell it, even the client can smell it. The atmosphere in the room changes, there is a positive feeling.***«

Physical awareness and the feelings associated with it offers a reliable tool in the evaluation of ideas. *John Hegarty:* »*I'm a great believer in what the heart feels today, the head knows tomorrow. Your emotions are a wonderful sensory device that nobody can put their finger on, nobody can touch it, nobody knows quite where it is ... it is all around you ... it's a thing that's there. The antennae are constantly sorting things all the time. That's about feel with your heart, listen to your heart.*«

What is the exact physical feeling that tells you, this is a Great Idea?

Separate Yourself from the Idea

Often, your individual perspective is not sufficient to evaluate whether your own work is good or bad. For this reason, many Top-Creatives distance themselves from their work, not just time-wise but also from its contents. That is not always easy. *Loz Simpson:* »*It's like ignoring a pain. If you have got a pain in your body, you can cut yourself off from it, or when someone is tickling your feet you can train yourself to ignore it. You come up to a point to forget things that you know about what you have just been working on and just look at the piece of paper.*«

Separate yourself from the work, you are only a medium for it and if the work is good it will win.

Marcello Serpa

When an idea is being evaluated individual values and preferences always come into the arena. This can hinder the evaluation. At this point you have to place your own person in the background and bring the work into the centre. *Andrew Cracknell:* »*I can tell you things that get in the way, too much ego, ulterior motives. You have to empty your mind of every motive.*«

Marcello Serpa: »*Separate yourself from the work, you are only a medium for it and if the work is good it will win.*«

The Creative Director should therefore keep a natural distance from the job. This allows him to recognize ideas that others oversee. This becomes clear in the example of the team that almost didn't recognize the idea "Good versus Evil" for Nike. *Bob Moore:* »*They had a huge range of ideas. It was the fourth of four ideas they had. They liked the other three better and they said, 'well we've got this other idea, – we don't like it, – do you want it'? We had to pull it out of them.*«

How could you evaluate your idea more objectively?

Have the Idea Checked by Creatives You Respect

When you are still feeling a bit uncertain if your idea is really great or not, it can be helpful to qualify your own standpoint and to test if the idea generates the same amount of energy for other people as it does for you yourself. *Steve Simpson:* »*I take ideas to people I respect and just lay them out and ask them what they think about it. You have to be willing to listen to them, you can't just take an idea to somebody you respect and just expect approval for it. You have to be ready to listen to some hard truth about it.*«

In order to be able to take criticism, it is important that the people making the criticism are completely accepted. *Xavi Garcias:* »*It's very important for me to get criticism from very good people, people who I respect a great deal. You can't learn from everybody, you can only learn from the best.*«

Such a Creative to check your work with, does not even have to work in the same agency as you. *Matthias Freuler:* »*I look at the ad and then I think, if he were to look at it now, would he say, great guy, or would he think that's shit. Usually it is the copywriter who doesn't work here.*«

It's very important for me to get criticism from very good people, people who I respect a great deal.

Xavi Garcias

Xavi Garcias: »*It's only important to respect the people you know are better than you. That's the way you learn and you grow. Not all opinions are constructive and correct.*«

Could you present your idea to a Top-Creative of your choice full of pride?

Check the Surprise Factor of the Idea

With the demand that the idea should surprise and generate new perceptions, Top-Creatives expect from their employees that the idea resists the usual.

Gilbert Scher: »*Don't try to make something you are sure to sell to me. Try to make something which is going to surprise me because if you show me something I can do myself I will not agree with that. I need to be surprised each time, because you are sure to stay enthusiastic.*«

Checking for the surprise is the test as to whether the idea is really new or not. Remember, the energy of the surprise is the energy of the idea. Milka Pogliani: »*Try to suprise me. When they start to tell me a story on a commercial, if after 5 seconds I can tell them how goes the ending something is wrong because it's so expected.*«

What would make your idea more surprising, more unexpected?

Expect Risks and Manage Them

New ideas break rules and challenge existing systems. Sometimes they move in areas where you have to deal with legal resistance. For the campaign in FACTS Magazine, Switzerland, in which the contents of famous peoples' bags were x-rayed, this risk was taken very consciously. *Matthias Freuler: »We set up a special war-fund so that we could pay legal claims. We live with the fact that maybe we would be sued; we did it exactly as we wished. In the meantime 11 sujets issues have been published and each one is a little bit more risky than the former one, but nothing has happened, as yet.«*

Taking the risk is the safest thing to do.

Bob Isherwood

We cannot expect to come up with something new and to be 100 per cent sure that we won't offend anybody. *Bob Isherwood: »Taking the risk is the safest thing to do. Originality implies no precedent, so you can be very unsure because what you have got is an idea that hasn't been done before. Usually the biggest risk lies in the ideas that are predictable, because ideas that are predictable don't get noticed. You can't sell anything to anyone unless they notice you.«*

What are the biggest risks of the idea that you should consciously manage?

Don't take Criticism of the Idea Personally

Only when we have separated ourselves from the idea, we are able to hold onto or to reject it, independent of our own energy. If you identify too strongly with your idea, you will take it as a

personal attack if the idea is criticised. This is not a good position for a defence. In order to be flexible and to protect the idea from all sides, we have to detach ourselves from the idea.

Mike Wells: »**Once you've had the idea, then you must be big enough to let other people have an input because they might improve it. It's very hard especially, when a junior starts working. When you put a piece of work up on the wall, people think they're putting themselves up there. You have to divorce yourself from that and not take offence when someone criticises it.**«

You will be very inflexible in dealing with an idea you fell in love with.

Are you open and flexible enough to take on criticism and improvements from others easily?

Look at Doubts on the Feasibility of the Idea as Something Positive

Whether an idea is surprising and so really challenging, can also be seen in the reaction of other people. *Nick Worthington:* »**One of the surer signs is if you've got a piece of work on your wall and people come up and say, 'You'd never be able to do that.' That's a good sign. 'No, they would never buy that.' That's usually a good sign.**«

'You'd never be able to do that.' That's a good sign.
'No, they would never buy that.'
That's usually a good sign.

Nick Worthington

Uncertainty is a definite sign that the idea is not a well known yet and new. *Marcello Serpa:* **»There are two types of ideas. The certain idea that goes click or the crazy idea that is either brilliant or a complete flop.«**

Maybe it is pride that motivates us at this point to make the impossible possible. It helps us to show others that we ourselves, and the idea, are better than other people think.

Is the idea challenging enough to arouse doubts on the feasibility of the idea?

Evaluate the Idea Beyond the Target Group

A Great Idea goes far above and beyond the actual assignment. That is what makes a "Big Idea" so great.

Felix de Castro: **»It should be brilliant, both to the people you are addressing and to those you are not addressing. You should try and make most people who see it glad of having seen it, or at least interested in having seen it.«**

It should be brilliant, both to the people you are addressing and to those you are not addressing.

Felix de Castro

In best cases Great Ideas, successful ideas, even become the talk of the town. They excite far more people than was intended. The reason is, that people have more in common than they have differences. That also builds the basis for the international adaptation of ideas. Top-Creatives therefore

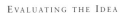

focus their evaluation right from the start on whether the idea is liked by people in general, and not just by the target group.

Does the idea also excite people outside the target group?

Kill your "Baby" Yourself Before Others do it

In order to check whether the idea has been carefully processed and if it meets all the requirements, you should try to "kill" it. This is basically the durability test for an idea. With this method Top-Creatives quickly find out what problems they could possibly have with the idea. In addition, it is easier to kill your own idea yourself than to have others do it for you. *Rob Kitchen: »I suppose it's like chucking it into the swimming pool and seeing if it swims or drowns.«*

Rob Kitchen

An idea that survives this test is most likely a strong idea. If, on the other hand, it can be wounded, we should figure out from the start how to change the idea at this point and to make it bullet-proof. *Rob Kitchen: »That's a really important part of the process. It's to try to pick holes in it, and not enough people do it. If you kill your own baby, then that's your choice. But if somebody else does it, you get very upset. You have to try to kill it, and if it still lives, then it's obviously a very strong baby.«*

Sooner or later the Account Manager, the Creative Director or the client will try to attack the idea. Its up to you to strengthen the strong points of the idea and to reduce its weaknesses.

Jon Matthews: »**Don't give up until you really get a strong idea. Throwing away stuff, being really prepared to throw away stuff, I think you have to be. Just get round to burn your babies.**«

Question your idea, find weaknesses and be its biggest critic.

> *What justified objection can kill your idea immediately and what would certainly make it stronger?*

Keep At It, Don't Give Up

A Top-Creative plays longer and more determined than other Creatives. Or, in other words: many Creatives give up too soon. The fact that the job has to be handed in on a particular deadline, makes many Creatives satisfied too early. They believe that it is better to have something rather than nothing. This is dangerous, because once this thought has set in, it ensures that, from now on, you will occupy yourself with the execution of a "good" rather than a "very good" solution.

Keep going, when others give up and go home. Stay dissatisfied when others are satisfied. The bite is decisive for the better idea, far more than talent is. *Donna Weinheim:* »**It has helped me so many times, more than inspiration or genius. I don't give up and I keep going on and on till I do get it. Believe me, there are times when a week could go by where there are terrible ideas. But I don't just want to give up, and that is what's helped me.**«

It's almost like a torture, self-inflicted torture.

Nick Worthington

This means that you don't have to be genius to have a Great Idea, but you have to be prepared to work hard for it. It almost seems as if the pressure and the suffering before an idea shows up is

important, so that afterwards the solution is also experienced as a "relief". *Nick Worthington:* »*It's almost like a torture, self-inflicted torture.*«

Does the idea really fulfil your highest standards,
or are you already giving up?

Don't Evaluate the Idea Until the Next Day

As long as we are still under the influence of the physical energy of an idea, we are hardly in a position to have an objective opinion. You have to separate yourself first and then you have the requirements necessary for an open, flexible and unprejudiced evaluation. *Marcello Serpa: »I separate the whole thing. I detach myself and draw loads of scribbles. And a day later I look at it and say yes, I will do it, no, I won't do it.*«

When a good idea appears everybody feels very excited.
I want to do it now, it's great and it's better
to leave things for one or for two days.

Hernan Ponce

With the detachment of a whole night, you can usually see the work more clearly, which will make it easier to evaluate more objectively. Then you can see if the energy is actually manifested in the idea, or whether you have only felt your own energy.

Hernan Ponce: »When a good idea appears everybody feels very excited. I want to do it now, it's great and it's better to leave things for one or for two days. You are not so in contact with it

because in the process you are working you are very involved in the problem, involved in the solution, you know you need space, you need time, you need to separate from the idea.«

A distance of time is particularly worthwhile when you are working alone on a project.

Do you still think it is a Great Idea the next morning?

Check if the Idea Works on its Own

Instead of lots of words and explanations, Top-Creatives first check to see if the idea also functions on its own. It is going to have to do so sooner or later anyway. So they just leave it lying on the table and watch their colleagues looking at it for the first time. This is a realistic test where you can find out if the idea works and if it really provokes a reaction. *Kevin Flatt: »You know it is working when you put it in front of somebody else and just stand back, don't say a word and just see what they do and watch their reaction and if you get one of those 'oh, this is cool', that's when you know that it is working.«*

With this trick, Top-Creatives get a second "external first impression" because they want to be absolutely sure that their idea positively surprises. *Xavi Garcias: »I leave the campaign on the table, and when my colleagues enter and don't say anything, quite possibly I don't have a kiss. The colour of lipstick can go out-of-date, but the kiss will never do so.«*

Check your muse kiss before you present it to the wide masses so that you can limit any possible damages.

Do you get a strong reaction to your idea without any explanation?

142 Trust in Your First Reaction and Take the Consequences

With the first spontaneous evaluation of an idea you can overcome rational feelings that appear over time, and accordingly, train your instincts. *Gerard Stamp:* »*It's to believe in one's own instincts and first impressions, they're generally right. If you read something and you immediately think it's not very good, that's generally because it's not very good. You have to have the courage of your own instincts really, looking at something.*«

Remember, Great Ideas are supposed to work quickly in the market and be understandable. *Karel Beyen:* »*The really good ideas are really natural, simple or they're like you don't think much about it yourself. When it clicks in my head then I know that's good.*«

If you read something and you immediately think it's not very good, that's generally because it's not very good.

Gerard Stamp

"You never get a second chance to make a first impression" also holds true for ideas. *Dan Wieden:* »*The first reaction is probably the most powerful, did that move me, did that challenge me, did that effect my perception of things, or did that seem like a comfortable well designed thing? Personally I respond more to things that challenge where I am, and what my perceptions are.*«

Did it "click" immediately when you first looked at the idea?

143 Evaluate the Idea Quickly, as if You were under Time Pressure

Time pressure helps to overpower rationalisation. We experience this when, for example, an add has to be approved by the client very quickly, because it then is not going to be questioned or test-

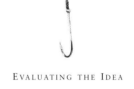

ed as much. Time pressure can also increase the quality of an idea. Because if you have to think over a decision for too long, then something is wrong. *Peter Seidler: »It's really much better to be showing things quickly, that's my pragmatic 'the dog grasp sticks' theory.«*

In a campaign for a Mexican restaurant, "Fresh TV" was produced every morning. It was filmed from 5 till 7 a.m. and it was edited from 9 till 10 a.m. Then the spot went on the air. *Steve Simpson: »If you are under time pressure and under the discipline of finding out what's an essential point, you're much more brutal and it's probably a good lesson to apply to your own work all the time.«*

I play the same standards if I am judging an award show.

Ted Sann

Also, the end user only has 2 to 3 seconds to let the idea take effect, just like the jury in Cannes. A quick evaluation of the idea is nothing other than an early real evaluation. *Susan Westre: »The jury went through it so fast, that unless it grabbed you in the first two seconds you know it was out. So one strategy for an award show is, something must be really catchy and grab you.«* That's why the perception in the market could also be called an award show that gives the idea an award by buying the product.

Ted Sann: »I play the same standards if I am judging an award show. You have to make sure you understand the idea and you have to give the idea a chance to breathe a little and then judge it.«

The aim is to switch off your own rational thoughts through the speed of the evaluation of the idea. *Karel Beyen: »Always do the judgement fairly quickly. Don't think about it, don't think about the client and don't think about nothing, just not have all those layers.«*

Do you evaluate the idea quickly enough to avoid rationalisation?

Test the Uniqueness of the Idea Based on Competition

One of the hardest tests for an idea is to replace the existing logo with a competitive logo and check to see if the ad still works. If the answer is yes, this is a sure sign that the communication idea is not unique. *Rich Silverstein: »I didn't approve any ad or commercial where you could've put another product into. I said it had to prove to me that it could only be done with a Polaroid – and that was my little test.«*

If you really identify with the product, you can also check if the idea is so great that you wouldn't want your competitor to have it. *Fernando Vega Olmos: »One thing I do is I put not the brand that I'm working for but the competitor in. Look what's going on with you, I hate it, I don't want to develop this for this brand of my competitor, okay then that's a good ad.«*

Rich Silverstein

The more specific an idea is, the less it will suit another brand. *Jon Moore: »You take that same situation, a little boy coming in and waking up his dad at 3.30 in the morning, going dad, dad, wake up, what is it? Dad, dad, you promised to take me to Taco Bell – clang – it doesn't work, it will only work with McDonald's, because McDonald's is institutionalised in people's minds that is an absolutely natural thing for the kid.«*

How could you give an idea an even more unique form?

Make an Idea-Wall in Your Room

You will always find good ideas, and others not too good, close to very good ideas. In order to tell the difference it is very helpful to give your ideas a clear structure so that you know exactly what their energy status is. Some Top-Creatives have wall sections in their rooms for this.

On the safe wall people go oh, that's a good spot, but no-one is going wow, we ought to shoot that.

Don Schneider and Michael Patti

Don Schneider and *Michael Patti:* »*There is a sure wall, there is the unsure wall and then at the back of the office is the death wall. Where an idea is that you want to be good but it's not presenting well and it's just fading away, that's the death wall. We just keep trying to work on them until we either kill them. On the good wall we have a spot working that every time you present it to each other or to anyone else gets a little better. An account guy comes in, you present it, he loves it, it gets a little better. On the safe wall people go oh, that's a good spot, but no-one is going wow, we ought to shoot that.*«

With this system your ideas will get a clearer status and can be processed more targeted.

With what method could you make your ideas internally public and improve them?

Evaluate the Idea in its Expected Environment

To realistically evaluate an idea, many Top-Creatives put themselves in the place of the consumer.

Ted Sann: »*First I react to it emotionally almost like a consumer watching this commercial and than I will make some intellectual judgements about its strategies, if it is making our points.*

I'm watching it the way I was watching a basketball game and a commercial came up how I would react to it. I'm almost trying to be a blank mind without thinking about this strategy.«

Judge it as it exists in the world next
to programming and next to editorial.

Steve Simpson

How meaningful the idea will be for people is a main concern for Top-Creatives. *Christian Vince: »I try to see a campaign as a consumer. I want to be interested by the message first. Because you are deeply in the life of the people on TV, everywhere, so you must enjoy them, give pleasure to these people, because you stop the film you have to give them something which is at least as interesting as a movie that you interrupted.«*

Steve Simpson: »Judge it as it exists in the world next to programming and next to editorial.«

*How could the idea be made even more exciting
and relevant for its editorial surrounding?*

Check if You Really and Truly Want to Execute the Idea

With Great Ideas you can hardly wait to see them happen. That is why you can recognize an unusual idea on this driving force. *Rich Silverstein: »You get this feeling that you can't wait to produce it, it's like I got it, oh it'll be great, I can't wait to photograph it.«*

This excitement and happy expectation is also a result of the energy of the idea and helps you to get other people involved, excited. From your team partner to the client and up to the Director. *Lee Garfinkel: »If already I have started thinking about who the director should be and I can't*

wait to see the film and I want to start getting in the editing room then it's a natural excitement that comes up because I think the spot's going to be very good.«

Michael Patti: »*You can't wait to get out and shoot it, you want to see it come to life.«* This energy can be very strong and intensive. *Bob Moore:* »*Where you have an idea that's so fun, or a sort of an idea when you can't get to sleep that night because you can't wait to get in to work in the morning so you can keep working on it.«*

On the other hand, the absence of this driving force can also be an indication that it is not a Great Idea.

Are you really keen on bringing the idea to life?

Check if You Want to See the Idea over and over again

You can look over the very best ideas over and over again. It is like a brilliant film, novel or book, with every perception we discover new small parts or aspects that touch us. A Great Idea is therefore substantial and offers many layers to enjoy. The desire to see an idea again and again, shows us that it is permanently energetic. *Donna Weinheim:* »*The best is when they want to see it again and again.«* This is also true for multi-media applications. *Kevin Flatt:* »*It should be a great experience and they should want to come back and do it again and again.«*

Only this reaction can turn a Great Idea into a classic. *Xavi Garcias:* »*The difference between a good and a bad thing in advertising is that the bad thing is old in three years, but a good thing in three years becomes a classic.«*

Do you want to see the idea over and over again,
regardless of fashion trends?

Check if the Idea Inspires You to many other Ideas

A Great Idea is full of energy. This inspires automatically to more ideas. For this reason, it is relatively easy for a great print or TV idea to be produced in another media and in many different forms.

Felix de Castro: »*I came back to the agency the day after and explained the idea to the rest and immediately came up with some other possibilities. Tons of different visuals.*«

Mike Wells

This energy also helps in the professional conversion of the idea, for example when an integrated approach is necessary in the market. Many Top-Creatives have therefore underlined that after the idea shows up, writing the ad or the commercial is almost automatic. *Mike Wells:* »***When you come up with a very simple idea, everything should write themselves. The commercial should write itself, the press ads should write itself, the posters should come. If it's very difficult and you're thinking non-stop, then the idea probably isn't right. It's quite a natural thing. The ideas just spark off it.***«

Does the present idea lead to many more motives or ideas for other media?

Even Question the Media Plan for a Great Idea

Sometimes the power of the idea develops better in another media than in what it was originally planned. In this case Top-Creatives sometimes put the idea above the media plan. In the end, what they want to do is to reach and excite people. And a media plan is as well only an "execution".

John Hunt: »*The brief came in and it was a print brief, it was meant to be a magazine ad and we couldn't come up with a decent magazine ad but we came up with a very nice TV idea. It was wonderful that we had a client we could go to and we showed him, and the client bought the TV idea. I always remember that because, if you like, it was born from the failure of a print idea.*«

When you're confronted with a Big Idea you've got to change the brief, the strategy, because the idea can be bigger than the strategy.

Gianfranco Marabelli

In order to demonstrate how easy it is to operate the power steering of a BMW, the team had a mouse run along the steering wheel. *John Hunt:* »*It was going to be a feather on the steering wheel that made it turn, and then it was going to be a butterfly, and then in the end we thought it would be fun if we could get a mouse to dance on a steering wheel.*«

As you can see, the power and energy of an idea really can influence the originally planned strategy and lead to it being changed. *Gianfranco Marabelli:* »*When you're confronted with a Big Idea you've got to change the brief, the strategy, because the idea can be bigger than the strategy.*«

Could the idea release more power in another media?

Refuse Bad Work

The most important word in the evaluation of an idea is "No!" because, in the end, most ideas are not really brilliant, they have received "Yes!" too many times, in form of compromises and concessions. *Toni Segarra:* »***The most difficult part of my job is to reject the work. That means, that 90 per cent of the time you need to reject the work because it's difficult to find brilliant work every day. It's difficult to say to the people, okay, this is shit and you need to work again on the process.***« In particular you need to do this with extreme sensitivity, so that you kill the idea, but not the motivation.

90 per cent of the time you need to reject the work because it's difficult to find brilliant work every day.

Toni Segarra

The power and consistency needed for this permanent rejection requires a strong motive. *Toni Segarra:* »*I don't want to leave any traces of bad work. I'm allergic to bad work. It's greater than my fear of telling people 'no', of rejecting ideas.*«

Ask yourself how you would feel if the work carried your name, would you still find it good? *Joe Duffy:* »*My name goes on everything so I want to make sure that I feel good about it.*«

For what strong personal motive would you reject bad work?

How to Let the Energy of an Idea Jump over:

Clients buy
conviction

At a presentation, the energy of an idea should jump over to other people. For this purpose
the idea should be light, without too many execution details. Most important however, is that those
who are presenting the idea are really and truly excited about it. This is catching, and provides
emotional security. In particular, when an idea is new and risky, it needs security from the people presenting it.
In case of doubt, it is the presenter's conviction and power that keeps the idea alive.

not an idea

Toni Segarra

The Presentation as the Moment when the Spark Jumps over

At the presentation of a Great Idea, the energy that was felt in the evaluation of the idea, should jump over to other people. The most dangerous part is the moment of surprise, when you present a new challenging perspective for the observer or the client. The presentation of this unusual part, which gets attention in the market, is often exactly why an idea gets killed in the presentation.

Xavi Garcias: »An idea is very fragile. A normal idea is more resistant than a very good idea. A very good idea is weaker. It's defenceless because nobody can perceive it. Its novelty is frightening.«

The more unusual an idea is, the more convincingly it will have to be presented. The client will feel if this conviction is real or missing. With most Creatives, this is actually missing because they are not 100 per cent convinced of the solution themselves. Maybe they actually sense or know that they are not delivering the best possible work, and that's why they are not totally behind it. Uncertainty spreads just as quickly as certainty. So the decision on the success of a presentation is made long before the presentation itself. And a presentation is only an execution means to sell the idea. And someone who is not excited about the idea he is presenting, should better not present it and cancel the presentation.

*Xavi Garcias: »**The worst thing that can happen to you is having a client that approves the campaign you don't like.**«*

That is why Top-Creatives operate much more directly and determined, and only present solutions that really excite them. The aim of the presentation is to transport the energy of the idea, that we ourselves have felt, so that others can feel it too, so that the spark jumps over. The more unusual an idea is, the more personal energy and powers of persuasion will be needed.

For that reason, Top-Creatives tend to present an idea reduced to one sentence, one scribble or as a key visual in order to focus on the person giving the presentation. *John Hunt: »**For TV we don't normally do storyboards, it's like just a big comic book, we just act it out and talk it through. We might have some reference points but I think that the client understands if you're passionate and**

enthusiastic.« Not going to far in-depth about the final production and execution details at the presentation saves time and money.

Instead, Top-Creatives have an absolutely clear vision of what they are selling.

Alexandra Taylor: »You have to have a vision of what you want because everybody around you will try to water it down, try to take it away from you. Try and make it less of it, and you have got to hold onto that vision and to what you want and not give up on it.«

It should be clear at this point why both the client and the agency should have a common vision of the standards demanded of the idea. They should not just basically agree that ideas are important, but also on what exactly distinguishes a very good from a just good idea. But even then, you can only bridge different opinions through mutual trust and respect.

Xavi Garcias: »The first thing is that you must believe in this idea, and that this is clear, visible, fundamental. You must transmit this confidence. Secondly, you need your client's absolute trust. If the client doesn't believe in the idea, at least he must believe in you.«

You can check whether your presentation allows a Great Idea to jump over easily by answering the following questions:

☆ Is there a clear mutual vision from the client and agency about the standards demanded of the Great Idea?
☆ Is there a precisely formulated and approved Creative Brief with which you can judge if the idea is on strategy?
☆ Are you presenting the idea in the shortest form, so that you really sell the idea and not the execution?
☆ Are you being courageous and concentrating on the one idea that you prefer, an idea that you chose with fullest conviction?

☆   Are you only showing your client solutions that really and truly excite you, and does this feeling come across?

If you can answer these questions with "yes", you will present unusual ideas lightly and with conviction. If not however, you will probably present many different ideas, instead of one Great Idea, and you will make your client so uncertain that he will probably decide on tests, or a combination of your ideas, and this usually leads to mediocre ideas. The following tips and questions will help you to effectively increase your powers of conviction.

Enthuse Different Clients with Different Ways of Presenting the Creative Energy

The client is also a target group that wants to be enthused. In order to let the energy of an idea jump over in the best possible way, the optimum presentation should always be tailored to the client. *P.J. Pereira: »I present it in the way that I believe that it will be the easiest way for them to buy it.«*

The greatest excitement for the client often comes from the powers of the Creative who has already physically felt the energy when the idea showed up. *John Hunt: »At Hunt Lascaris the creatives do the selling. We've some very good clients for who we can draw on the back of a matchbox and they would understand. For others we have to go through strategic presentation first, so it depends on the client.«* It is the excitement that counts, and pulls everybody along with it, and helps to overcome formal weaknesses.

Bob Moore: »I think creative people are very smart, sometimes they're shy, a lot of times they are very insecure, a lot of times they are not great, slick, presenters. I would rather have that person in the room explaining his or her idea then an account person saying 'Well this is what we are

doing here', I like having creative people stand up at a meeting and saying 'God-dammit, No this is what I want to do' and if they're passionate about it.«

I present it in the way that I believe that it will be the easiest way for them to buy it.

P.J. Pereira

A presentation by the Account Manager can also reach the target, provided he is more excited and more convincing. *Mike Wells: »To argue for your own ideas is quite difficult, because people are very shy of it. Where it's much easier to argue for someone else's idea if you are divorced away from it.*« The aim remains the same, to transport the excitement and the enthusiasm for the idea. For this reason, the following is valid for most Top-Creatives:

Ted Sann: »If a junior copy writer did the work, he will present it.«

Who can convey the most excitement for the idea?

Never Present Anything that You Still Question

The moment you question something you withdraw energy from it. *Jon Matthews: »I think, if it's not quite there yet we have lots of questions. If you question it it's not quite right yet. If you accept it without question that's the best stuff. I think that's true of anything, any piece of music or any film you watch, if you accept it without question, it's brilliant.*«

If, at the presentation, others begin to question your idea, the answers should be clear because you should have already asked these questions at the idea evaluation. *Richard Flintham: »If you spend long enough interrogating the idea at the beginning, you'll have spent four weeks, starting off*

going 'what about this'. When people try to deconstruct it; you know you have been there already.«

Gianfranco Marabelli

One important preparation for the presentation is to clarify the idea for so long, until all open questions are answered. For Top-Creatives, the Great Idea is always an idea that will be presented without any doubts.

*Gianfranco Marabelli: »**I think that when the idea is very strong, that everybody agrees. A really Great Idea jumps immediately.**«*

Is the idea selected for the presentation unquestionably great?

Fight for Your Convictions with Determination

A client doesn't buy ideas, he buys you and your convictions. You are the only connection that is visible and can be felt in the presentation. *Toni Segarra: »**Clients usually buy conviction, not an idea. I tend to think that the clients buy confidence, conviction from an agency, not campaigns. They need to feel convinced about the advertising and they need to feel that you're convinced about selling.**«*

Because others often influence our opinions, it is important to present a solution that you believe in, and where you have a clear point of view.

PRESENTING THE IDEA

Xavi Garcias: »When you have to convince so many people, you need a lot of personal pressure and tension to do good work, because the easiest option is saying that the most mediocre work always convinces everybody. It's easier to do mediocre work than to convince many people to do good work.«

It's easier to do mediocre work than to convince many people to do good work.

Xavi Garcias

A strong personal idea will also give you the strength for an argument in which you might have to fight. *Toni Segarra: »I fight very hard with the client and with anybody, until someone ends up on the floor.«*

Just how totally convinced are you of the quality of the idea?

Present only One Solution

If you are not sure which solution is the best, you should discard both of them. The possibility of having two equally Great Ideas is small against having two merely good ideas. *Johan Gulbranson: »Some creatives show the client, look here what we did and the whole wall is full of ideas. I always have one idea because one idea is best. Not if you're making eight films of course, then you have to have eight ideas, but if you are doing one commercial it's stupid to come up with two because you know which is best and what's not. Then you give the client the chance to pick out the worst one, which they will, because it's not so daring as the best one.«*

Top-Creatives select the best idea according to certain evaluation criteria before the presentation, and do not leave the selection to the client. In this way, they direct the attention in a presentation

directly to the favoured idea. *David Caballero: »Show only one solution. Sometimes I can explain the other option to show why I'm not using it, why I rejected it, so that the client can evaluate it for himself.«*

I always have one idea because one idea is best.

Johan Gulbranson

Every additional idea reduces this attention and the powers of persuasion. The presentation of several alternative ideas is always a sign of uncertainty towards the idea, or the client.

Do you have the courage to only present your favourite Top-Solution to the client?

Be Convincing with Your Personality

Top-Creatives consciously select presentation forms where their personality has some space. This is the only way one can feel that you are really one hundred per cent convinced about the idea. Trust the idea, instead of hiding behind a whole stack of production proposals. *Don Schneider: »I could never ever present a storyboard because the storyboard is paper and ink and what we are presenting is film, movement and sound and emotion and it isn't on this piece of paper. Don't ever find yourself in that position, because in frame 5 you're dead, they're looking at the board. What I do is I draw these key frames. I want them watching my eyes, and want them watching me as I create the scene. We've sold spots where we never have shown a picture.«*

At a presentation where the storyboard is completely worked out there is little freedom for a personally convincing presentation style. That's why Top-Creatives only present one key visual, or they simply describe the idea verbally.

Michael Patti: »We tend to get up and hold a frame and act it out a little bit. I'll be reading this, and he will be doing that. And the client is watching and imagining in his head what this will be like finished, because we are really acting it out. We're putting more personality into it than you'd ever get in a drawing.«

We've sold spots where we never have shown a picture.

Don Schneider

The personal powers of persuasion and the ease with which you can react to questions in this form of presentation, also gets the client to trust in the idea, and in the presenter.

In what form of presentation are you the most convincing?

Present the Story – without a Board

The storyboard visualises the images for the first time that up to now have develop freely in everyone's heads. Here, at the latest, the arguments will begin on how the idea is to be executed. For this reason, Top-Creatives avoid presenting the storyboard too soon because it presses the idea into a particular form. *Felix de Castro: »I very seldom present storyboards. I very seldom show drawings or visualizations of the idea to the client. I'd rather have the idea perfectly understood and subscribed by the client and then let the director visualize it with us. So that the client doesn't stick to details but with the general idea principles.«*

In this way, the visualisation process and the production process is kept open for small changes that can strengthen the idea, and you don't have to agree on every small detail with the client. *Felix de Castro: »I believe that if the general idea principles are fulfilled and satisfied by the*

final commercial, that should be all the discussion issues. Not if the shirt of the guy is blue or if they are in a pink painted room. I'd rather don't lose time with that. I believe that the rest should be left to expertise and the more skilled abilities of the photographer or commercials director or sound studio or whatever.«

It's extremely important for the client to grasp what it is
that you are trying to do before you show them how to do it.

Lars Bastholm

At the presentation, it is important that the idea, and not the execution is sold, which could sometimes cover up the fact that an idea is missing. This is particularly important for complex applications like ideas for multimedia. *Lars Bastholm: »It's extremely important for the client to grasp what it is that you are trying to do before you show them how to do it.«*

*In what type of presentation form would your idea
develop the most power?*

Only Present what You would Buy Yourself

Real power of persuasion is only generated if you yourself would buy what you want to sell. If this is not the case, Top-Creatives take the consequences.

Gilbert Scher: »One day I was presenting a storyboard to Citroën and I was turning the picture and realised that the story-board was not as good as I thought. Then during the presentation I said I'm sorry but it is not the one we have to do, I'm sorry, but I prefer to come back. I can't sell to the clients something I wouldn't buy.«

*If we don't have this conviction, we don't present,
we ask for more time.*

Angel Sanchez

Only when you are totally convinced of your own work, can you present it with emotional certainty. *Angel Sanchez: »There is a big difference between someone who sells you a campaign and someone who convinces or is convinced of an idea. The feeling of being convinced is, that any question that you ask yourself about this campaign, you don't find any weak points. Confidence is something that you notice when you're presenting the campaign to the client and this confidence is also noticed by the client. If we don't have this conviction, we don't present, we ask for more time.«*

Would you be prepared to invest your own money in the idea?

Re-schedule the Presentation if no Great Idea Exists

If you don't have a Great Idea you have no reason for a presentation, remember, the presentation is not a tool by itself, but rather a medium that serves the idea. *Xavi Garcias: »The most honest thing to do is to postpone the presentation and go to the client and tell him that what you've got is not good enough and ask for more time and tell him you need to have a clearer idea. The worst thing that can happen to you is having a client that approves a campaign you don't like.«*

Re-scheduling a presentation is a sign of a high quality standard for the client and should be seen in a positive light. *Ted Sann: »We will have clients phone up being upset that the work isn't here this week, but you develop relationship over time to say, we need another week. You've to be ready to fight those fights and the clients have to understand that this is the way to get the best possible work.«*

The additional time needed is used effectively and is not expensive. Compared to the Media Spending later, with which the Idea is often communicated for several million. *Gilbert Scher:* *»If you say let me have two days more, I think your client will be pleased because he says my agency is working on my product and sometimes when I do it the client says, if you want you can have one week more.«*

Even with new business presentations it is often possible to move the presentation date in favour of a better idea. Remember, you are always fighting exclusively for the best idea.

Is the idea really good enough to approve its presentation?

Separate the Strategy Presentation from the Idea Presentation

The presentation of the strategy and the idea at the same time is very risky. The sale of a Great Idea requires an approved strategy, so that you are able to evaluate if the idea is on strategy. You cannot completely trust a strategy that has not yet been sold. This weakens your inner conviction.

Agreeing the strategy is eliminating possible risk factors for the creative part of the process.

Felix de Castro

You have to believe in two things now: the strategy and the idea. If the client is not in complete agreement with the strategy, your idea will be on shaky ground. If the client kills the strategy, your idea will be dead. Top-Creatives convince their clients of the strategy before the presentation. Then they feel secure in the discussion – in particular with unusual ideas. *Felix de Castro:* *»Without understanding or having a good strategy, you can't go anywhere. Because it's what worries the client most. To me, agreeing the strategy is eliminating possible risk factors for the*

creative part of the process. If you make sure that the client gets your idea of what the product needs is strategically right and fits in the product needs, the confidence in all the other issues will be higher and then they'll let you work with less limitations.«

A Great Idea is often the result of complex thought processes that the client should be made aware of. *Steve Simpson: »I think, the best way to sell it to the client is to invite him into your thought-process. Let them know that you didn't just come up with the idea off the top of your head, that a lot of thought had gone into it. And a lot of the assumptions were made along the way.«*

Have you already won the Strategy-Presentation for your idea?

Develop Ideas against Defence Reactions

Unusual solutions can be shocking in the presentation because Great Ideas are usually reduced to the minimum, and are often so powerful that the client cannot deal with their energy.
Bob Mackall: »It's something that he's never seen before but you've been with it for a month or 6 weeks, you've it all figured out, its strengths, its weaknesses and now – boom – you present it and you would like to have him react immediately and correctly and positively of course.«

Top-Creatives always expect a defence reaction and prepare for it. *Matthias Freuler: »It is almost always far, far, more difficult to sell the good ideas then the half-good ideas. That's why we get together and try to figure out what the objections will be. How can we persuade the client, how can we turn his objections into something positive? That is usually the final Creative Work.«*

A defence reaction came during a presentation for the magazine FACTS: *Matthias Freuler: »After-wards the client says, that is very dangerous, we will have X numbers of cancellations. And then you have to be able to argue with the client and say, yes there will probably be 100 or 200*

cancellations, but on the other hand, X-thousand will be impressed with what we are saying. This means going at the clients fear from the positive side.«

With what arguments could you fight
defence reactions to your idea?

Don't Think You Know what the Client will Buy

In one company you usually find several "clients" and everyone of them can all kill the idea, but only one person has the power to approve the idea. The problem is that it is very seldom that the idea is "bought with one hundred per cent conviction".

Sometimes when you make crazy, wild, creative work and we think the client isn't going to accept it they accept it and think it's fantastic.

Ramon Roda

Very often, the agency directors buy what they believe the client will buy, and then the client buys what he believes his Top-Management will buy. Because the idea has not been convincingly bought by anybody, it cannot be convincingly sold later. And we can easily be wrong in what we believe. *Ramon Roda: »Sometimes when you make crazy, wild, creative work and we think the client isn't going to accept it they accept it and think it's fantastic.«*

This is also true when we believe we have to present several ideas, so that we have one that the client can kill, or to show how busy we were. Here again, our beliefs can be a stumbling block for the chosen idea.

Milka Pogliani: »*Never go to see the client with average ideas because they are going to buy them, they feel safe and they are going to buy them.*«

What limiting assumption do you have of your client's taste?

Look at Every "Killed Idea" as a New Chance

All visible work is an idea that somebody somewhere accepted. But just because the client buys an idea doesn't mean it is good. On the contrary, sometimes it would be better if we had not sold an idea or a campaign, so that we could have developed something better.

Rich Silverstein: »*If I don't get to sell it, in some ways I believe there's another idea that wants to come out.*«

The quicker we transform difficult experiences, by discovering a meaning in them, the shorter the suffering period will be, and the quicker we will then be productive again. Sometimes a rejection simply means that the client has higher standards than we do. *Nick Worthington:* »*Sometimes clients will not buy a piece of work because it's not creative enough, not exciting enough, which is pretty good.*«

If I don't get to sell it, in some ways I believe there's another idea that wants to come out.

Rich Silverstein

Top-Creatives are more motivated by the client's high standards than by the frustration of losing an idea. *Joe Duffy:* »*Back to the drawing board, you have to pick yourself up and say, okay,*

I know we can come up with another idea that takes into consideration the client's concerns and that we will be just as happy with. Nine times out of ten when we do that we come up with something better.«

Angel Sanchez

Some Top-Creatives even use their disappointment to develop creative passion from their anger and gain energy. *Angel Sanchez:* »*It's an act of fury. It's like a scorpion. It's like when the scorpion is in that ring of fire it injects its own poison and kills himself. It must come out of your most aggressive, your most fighting spirit. What you have to do is fill yourself with craziness, with passion to do something better.«*

What better idea can you present following a rejection?

Look for a Better Idea After the Presentation

Top-Creatives always fight for the best idea – even if they have already sold a very good one. That's why they are Top-Creatives. Often you think of a better idea just after a successful presentation. This is made easier because things are less tense, and you have let go of the problem, which opens new perspectives.

Chevy's Mexican Restaurant had gone to the agency to get more attention focussed on their stock exchange listing in the market. *Steve Simpson:* »*We already had a campaign that was presented to them which they liked, and Rich Silverstein was not sure that there was not a better idea out*

there ... so he asked me just to think about it ... I was simply shooting baskets and then some-thing clicked and it was interesting and we ended up producing it.«

It is only when you are totally committed to the best idea, that you have the power to conduct these types of risky client manoeuvres, because of course, this also endangers the idea that has already been sold. This kind of post-presentation can also motivate you to improve your execution idea.

*Which better idea can you present
after you have successfully sold your idea?*

How to Protect a Great Idea before it Shows up:

Belief

Our beliefs give things energy and substance. This is also true for the Great Idea –
from the first briefing up to production. That's why the protection of an idea begins way before
the idea shows up, with what we believe about the Creative Process, and the idea. Our
belief in the product, the target group, the client, and in ourselves, influences whether
we can protect a Great Idea and manifest it in the best possible way.

comes first

John Hegarty

Protection of the Idea and what do You Really Believe about Ideas?

Top-Creatives protect their ideas holistically. From the first meeting with the client, up to preparing the idea, through the evaluation and on to the presentation and production of the idea. For them, protecting the idea is not something passive, it's something very active; because you can lose the energy of an idea before you are even aware of it. All you need for example is a wrong briefing, an unclear strategy or people around you who are very fearful.

The best ideas were probably never produced because they were not properly prepared, evaluated, checked or protected. Or they showed up in surroundings that never wanted a really Great Idea. Just working with a client who is not really interested in a Great Idea, can kill the seed of an idea, – long before it actually "shows up", and for long afterwards – without this ever being really noticeable.

John Hegarty: »The easiest thing to do is to destroy a good idea. Somebody can compromise it, they can try and pervert it, they can misunderstand it, they can execute it badly, it needs care, love and attention and as far as television is concerned, the script is just the beginning of a journey.«

Good protection of ideas is also securely tied to the company in which the Creative Process is carried out. Top-Creatives protect the ideas during every phase of the Creative Process, in particular, with what they believe about the process and ideas.

»Ideas are the most fragile thing on earth.«
Felix de Castro

The knowledge of this fragility makes Top-Creatives even more sensitive and aware, so they can locate and recognize dangers before they can do any harm. But also protecting an idea too much can be dangerous. *Toni Segarra: »You need to protect ideas, but you need to improve them too. And in the process to improve, you could kill them. I think it's the hardest part of our work.«*

The protection of the idea is as important to Top-Creatives as the idea itself, because the idea can die in many places. Indifference, doubts, a disdainful look, a few de-motivating words are enough to kill an idea. So you have to believe in the idea to protect it, and make sure it is not destroyed or wounded.

This belief in the Great Idea keeps the energy alive in every phase of the Creative Process. Faith moves mountains, and convictions release new powers.

For example: If you really believe you cannot achieve something, you will never even try to go after it, and for this reason alone, you will not reach your target. If on the other hand, you believe you are one of the best, you will always make an extra effort and be highly motivated to continue to maintain this standard by giving your best. Do you believe you could actually win the Grand Prix in Cannes?

John Hegarty: »Once I believed it, I could do it. You can't wait for the proof before you can believe it, that's the trick. Belief comes first!«

Belief is most important because in the beginning, the form of a Great Idea is more like an assumption, or hope.

Protecting a Great Idea means protecting the Creative Process.

Hernan Ponce: »You have to protect ideas from the beginning to the end. When you present it to the client, when you pre-test it, when you choose the right production company and the right director, when you are doing the shooting, when you edit the commercials and so on. So you have to protect an idea all over the process.«

Whatever Top-Creatives believe about the Creative Process makes it easier for Great Ideas to show up. It increases creative performance, strengthens resistance power and increases self-esteem. This

also allows Top-Creatives to overcome critical incidents during the Creative Process and to influence them positively; this then generates many more unusual ideas.

Using the following questions you can check if what you believe about ideas generates the best conditions for the Creative Process:

☆ Do you believe that consciously managed processes can support you in finding
   Great Ideas?
☆ Do you believe that the process can influence the quality of an idea before it even
   becomes perceptible?
☆ Do you believe that you can win the Grand Prix in Cannes with your team?
☆ Do you believe that your Target Group is intelligent enough to understand highly
   demanding ideas?
☆ Do you believe that you can rely on your team partner completely, and that you can
   always relax yourself?

If you can answer the above-mentioned questions with "yes", you already have an easy and inspiring workflow in your working area. If not however, your doubts will take energy away from you and others that could be used for the development of Great Ideas. The following tips and questions will help you to better protect your energy, and your ideas, at the process and content level.

Be Aware of Your Thoughts

Be aware of the thoughts with which you give your idea power or withdraw power from it. Remember, the right thoughts not only move mountains, they also overcome hindrances in the Flow Process. Top-Creatives believe very effectively. It is their belief that gives them the energy to overcome boundaries. *John Hegarty: »**If you are full of doubt, it is too draining, it just takes up time, that could be thinking time. It's like a resource that you have got that you haven't got anymore.**«*

Every thought is a tool powered by a belief in something. This belief in things, ideas or people, gives these things, ideas or people power. Do you believe you can positively influence an idea showing up? What do you believe about the idea, the team, the client, the brand for which you are working? Do you believe that under the given circumstances you could win a Grand Prix in Cannes?

If you are full of doubt, it is too draining, it just
takes up time, that could be thinking time.

John Hegarty

John Hegarty: »**You have to believe in it. You can add up all the logical things, but ultimately you have to have a faith in it and say, I just sense this could be great, and then it's getting people to buy into that aspect.**«

In what phase do you begin to protect
the existence of a Great Idea?

Make the Creative Process Your Best Creative Partner

The belief in the Creative Process gives many Top-Creatives the security that the showing up of an idea does not depend on them exclusively. This also relieves tension. *Erik Voser:* »**I believe that a good idea does not come of its own accord. I believe the key to a good campaign is the preparation for the arrival of an idea, regardless of what condition I am in.**«

A lack of good ideas can therefore be a result of something lacking in the preparation process, and can be improved at any time. *Mike Wells:* »**Everything can always be improved and you never stop doing that.**«

The belief in the continued improvement keeps the process running, and ensures constant optimisation. The more we let ourselves become a victim to this process, instead of managing it, the less we will be able to increase our creative performance. The role of the victim is a wound through which we lose energy, and which we cannot close because others are responsible for it. Then it is the fault of the client, the product, the briefing, the time, the circumstances etc.

Everything can always be improved and you never stop doing that.

Mike Wells

It is only when we accept responsibility for what is happening, that we are able to change it. The awareness that it is always we, ourselves, that stand in the way of the idea, helps us to accept more responsibility for the Creative Process, and also for whatever is blocking the Creative Process. *Enrico Bonomini: »I think the creative block is a part of the Creative Process, it's a part of you.«*

Are you working decisively on the steady improvement of the Creative Process?

Maintain Your Vision

If the belief in your own idea is strong enough, it can also be maintained over a long time period. This is important, because sometimes the time is not ripe for a Great Idea, and it has to be presented again and again until it can be sold.

The "Drugstore" idea for Levi's was introduced by the team from Nick Worthington and John Gorse again and again, until it was finally produced after ten years, and then went on to get gold

The best creative people are optimists
John Hegarty
because they always believe the impossible.

in Cannes, and lots of attention for the product and the brand in the market. *Nick Worthington:* »*Drugstore, we tried to get it introduced pretty much every year. There was a lot of internal resistance at the agency to it. Not from John Hegarty, but from other people at the agency who were really worried about the kind of overt sexual nature of it, just because it was about a guy taking a girl out, and he was going to have sex with her. That was all it was about. We made it ten years after we wrote it.*«

John Hegarty: »*The best creative people are optimists because they always believe the impossible.*« It is the belief that makes the impossible possible.

> *Are you so convinced of your idea*
> *that you would present it every year,*
> *again and again?*

Keep Your Belief in the Idea

Whatever it is that makes an idea attractive to people, also makes it attractive to other "matter" and clutter, which could weaken its energy. Every superfluous not important detail diverts attention from the actual idea and message.

Susan Westre: »*A lot of it is protecting an idea, is trying to convince the people involved along the way that simplicity is the right thing to do because what clients try to do is they want to put too many things into an ad or into a TV spot.*« Everything that does not strengthen an idea, automatically makes it weaker.

One perfect example of just how much you have to believe in the clarity of an idea, in order to maintain its quality, is displayed by the print and poster motive for "Skidmarks" for the Mercedes SLK, that won a Grand Prix in Cannes. *Gerard Stamp: »**The client was thinking people won't quite understand this, so should we not think of adding a headline like, 'It'll stop you in your tracks'. Now as soon as you put a headline on there that says something like that, it's dead, it's ruined, it's completely destroyed. Because the great thing about this, is that you leave a little bit of jigsaw for the viewer to fill in, you allow the viewer a bit of intelligence to complete the picture for them.**«*

In this case, the belief in the intelligence of the observer is protective of the idea. Just the same as a trusting cooperation between the client and the agency. *Gerard Stamp: »**The client knows that nothing would run that the agency would not be happy to run. So if he was insisting that there would be a headline that we would have had to take the ad off the table altogether.**«* Every creative should always be aware that he couldn't be forced to execute bad work.

How strongly do you believe in your idea?

Trust and Follow the Idea

Sometimes, we ourselves are the most dangerous idea killers. Pressure of performance, being over-critical, lack of time or lack of imagination can be dangerous to the idea when it shows up, so that it has to be protected from you, yourself.

I don't know if I came up with the ideas or
the ideas came up with me.

P.J. Pereira

Matthias Freuler: »It starts with yourself, that you repress the things that are coming into your mind, because you are telling yourself you can't.«

Therefore, a nurturing environment is the best support for an idea, because we really don't know how much of this idea comes from ourselves, or from others. *P.J. Pereira: »I don't know if I came up with the ideas or the ideas came up with me. I think the big point is inspire people and get inspired by them. Create an inspiring environment for everybody.«*

It starts with yourself, that you repress the things that are coming into your mind, because you are telling yourself you can't.

Matthias Freuler

It is helpful to put your ego in the background and to follow the idea. *Jeff Goodby: »Sometimes you just have to go to where an idea leads you and play it out and see whether you think it worked and not listen to other people.«*

Where will the idea lead you if you follow it trustfully?

Don't Show Your Idea too Soon

Young ideas are usually still too weak and immature. *Erik Voser: »The danger is to show the idea too soon because then it will definitely be killed and it is difficult to present it again afterwards. Before we show an idea we have to check if it is the right one and develop it into a Big Idea.«*

The energy of an idea is comparable to a fire starting to burn. *Fernando Vega Olmos:* »**An idea is a very fragile thing at the beginning. It's like, when the fire is big it is not so easy to extinguish it, when the fire begins it is very easy to extinguish so you have to keep in touch with the idea and try to protect it by fighting, I'm a good fighter.**«

When the fire begins it is very easy to extinguish.

Fernando Vega Olmos

Accordingly, an idea has to be stable so that at least, we ourselves know what we are fighting for. *Juan Gallardo:* »**I make sure that the idea is solid, that I have answers for every criticism that might come up. To be a complete salesman, if I have an idea I want to sell it. In order for me to sell it I have to anticipate what the problems might be that will see, and so that's how we approach things now.**«

Is your idea stable enough for a presentation?

Let the Seed of the Idea Grow Slowly

The development of a Great Idea is a balance between control and freedom that is granted. Just like the growing up of a living creature. *Mike Wells:* »**It's like a parent with a child, you protect it, but if you protect it too much then it won't grow. It might actually be a crap idea, but you've to be open that it still might be great.**«

For this reason, Top-Creatives constantly protect the seed of the idea, not the form that is already visible. *Toni Segarra:* »**I try to understand the essence of the ad, rather than not to lose it. But it's very difficult.**«

Only when you understand the essence, will you be able to protect it. If you don't understand it, you will hold on to its form and hinder its growth. If in doubt, it helps to keep the vision of the idea open for a longer time.

I don't conceive ideas, I don't create ideas, I develop them.

Marcello Siqueira

Chuck Carlson: »It always pays to expand your vision and try to see a lot of ideas before you focus down.«

What would allow the essence of the idea that you want to develop grow slowly?

Fight for the Idea and not just for the Visual or the Headline

If a client kills an idea, it is important to record exactly what was not bought. Maybe it is a simple execution detail, or only some words in a headline why the idea was killed. The exact differentiation of all elements an idea is made of can help to keep it alive.

Javi Carro: »You can't lose an idea. I have had cases, where you have lost a title, a specific sentence or a specific headline, but not an idea. So you lose a headline or a visual, but not an idea.«

A strong concept of an idea is not dependent on a single image or headline. Instead of throwing away the whole concept, Top-Creatives think about how to hold onto the idea but to express it

differently. This means that an attack on the Sujet (image or headline) will not be seen as an attack on the whole concept, and the chances of keeping the idea alive are increased.

You can't lose an idea. So you lose a headline or a visual, but not an idea.

Javi Carro

You have to clearly differentiate between the Execution of the Idea and the Higher Concept of the idea. You then also have to be clear about, what the difference is between the Higher Concept and the Benefit Idea – the strategic direction of the message.

What is the Higher Concept of your idea that should be protected?

Keep your Idea at the Highest Possible Energy Level

Top-Creatives push the energy of an idea to the edge, to a point where it can only get worse. *Richard Flintham:* »*We'll take it up to that level there and then meet somebody there, and then let's just leave the last little bit to make it five per cent better, or a few per cent better. We'll take the idea up to a certain point and that's a point that we won't allow the idea to go back from.*«

Remembering the feeling you had when the idea showed up provides you with important orientation. *John Hegarty:* »*If you have a vision for where this idea is going then just hold onto that vision constantly. Always go back to how it started, where it started, what was the feeling you had when you had that idea, lock yourself into that. You have got to stay true to what the idea was.*«

We'll take the idea up to a certain point and that's a point that we won't allow the idea to go back from.

Richard Flintham

This behaviour is particularly important in front of the client. *Jon Moore: »I've had clients who were great at buying good work and then you go through the editorial process and then they find the idea in the spot and they'd go: There is the one thing that's bothering me about this, can you take that out. But the difference between a successful team and an unsuccessful team or creative person is just the willingness to stick to it.«*

Does the idea still meet your high standards?

Defend the Idea, even against Small Bad Changes

Sometimes it is not the whole idea that is killed but instead a few "small improvement proposals" are offered, which actually make the idea worse, because it was not understood correctly, or because the consequences of these changes have not been taken into account. You have to be highly alert at this point because instead of a half-baked improvement of the idea, Top-Creatives would prefer to make a decisive change rather than an ongoing compromise, which slowly weakens the idea.

Richard Flintham: »We are really protective of ideas. Against people making them half a per cent worse than they are, so they say, Oh your idea is nearly through we've just got to change it that little bit, and if it makes it a little bit worse then you shouldn't do it. We just say what's the point in making it worse.«

*We are really protective of ideas. Against people
making them half a per cent worse than they are.*

Richard Flintham

Ignoring problems or difficulties does not help either. The active handling of the idea is important so that it remains alive. *Rob Kitchen: »Sometimes it means there are too many problems with it, so it doesn't work, but other times just by changing a couple of words, or maybe shooting it from a different angle, they're often solvable. You have to make sure whoever comes along doesn't think it's a crap idea, right from the start.«*

How can you improve the modification requests
made on your idea?

Defend the Idea against Compromises with Determination

Often, the danger is not that the idea will be killed at once, but rather that it will die slowly because of small concessions made bit by bit.

Jeff Goodby: »Eventually you start making lots of little changes and you don't even notice what's happening to the project. The best thing to do is to just kill the thing yourself, like if the client is asking for something that you think is really likely to be hurtful to the project. One of the best things to do is to just say to them, 'listen, I don't think this is really where we should go', you're not comfortable with it, let's start over.«

Sometime this means that the client will then accept the idea. But it is always better to start with a new idea than to make it "normal". *Bob Mackall: »Keep people from turning a good idea into something that they are more familiar with, something that they're more comfortable with.«*

Jon Moore: »A lot of it has to do with really protecting the idea what it's about, and understanding it and then being very tough about not letting it get watered down or kind of like taken off track along the way.«

What better solution do you have instead of a compromise?

Be Dissatisfied with Your Last Performance

Top-Creatives do not compete against others but against themselves. They learn more quickly from their mistakes, take the consequences and increase their standards regularly. *Michael Patti: »The key element is the desire not to fail, and to be better than you were the last time and trying not to quit until you at least feel that you've done that. I'm always afraid of failing and I think that helps keep me pumped to make sure I won't.«*

I have never done my best work.

Rich Silverstein

The attitude of Top-Creatives does not allow much space for mediocrity. *Milka Pogliani: »Don't think, you have got the best.«* This is true both for the work of others and your own work. *Rich Silverstein: »I have never done my best work.«*

Every day offers you a new, better chance. Even if the best work of all cannot be done immediately and every day. *Steve Simpson: »Ultimately you'll do something that's better than average and hopefully really good. But it may not be today.«*

How satisfied are you with your work today?

Keep Your Cool in the Find the Idea Phase

Belief can relax you and contribute enormously to an idea showing up. If you keep cool you will let ideas simply show up – without any difficulty.

Some days you go fishing and there's nothing out there, is that your fault?

Dan Wieden

Dan Wieden: »*In order to come up with good ideas I think you have to believe they will be given to you. I don't have ideas, they will be given to me.*«

This kind of trust has very broad consequences. *Dan Wieden:* »*For me it's very much a trust. I always had this little agreement, I will not take complete credit for what I do. If I also don't have to take complete blame for what I don't. Some days you go fishing and there's nothing out there, is that your fault? Maybe, maybe not, but the conscious mind is not the only thing involved in the creation of good work.*«

You have to do your homework first in order to really "Catch Big Fish", the Creative Brief should supply the springboard for this. Good preparation relaxes you, not just in the Finding of an Idea.

Could it be that the idea finds you?

Believe in Yourself

Self-confidence is important to be able to judge processes and performance in the Creative Process independently of others. It is also important to guide other people with unusual ideas a step into the future.

John Hegarty: »If you don't believe in yourself, why should somebody else? And you are trying to convert people. Often an idea isn't obvious, it is often your enthusiasm that can make it happen, you must never deny that. That is part of what a creative person has to install in themselves: the ability to be able to go out and enthuse others, because other people have to buy into it who then also help to take the idea on.«

If you don't believe in yourself,

John Hegarty

why should somebody else?

This self-confidence is particularly important when the idea is in danger of getting lost. *Lee Garfinkel: »You've to believe in your concept and believe that you can do it. It's easy to lose confidence in yourself. Like in sports, if you start getting behind the other team you start thinking, you know we're not going to win this game, you psyche yourself out of winning.«*

Can you hold on to your energy in every situation?

Be a Good Idea Consultant

Top-Creatives are Top-Consultants. They advise in the sense of what is new, and manage the idea and the process professionally. If you cannot equally well consult and have ideas, you will most likely be out of place in the creative economic field. Train your consulting qualities. *Jon Matthews: »If you are only just a pure creative then don't go and get a job in advertising, go to be an artist, because we are commercial people.«*

Excluding the advisory function in the creative field leads very quickly to handicaps in selling and protecting Great Ideas. The more unusual an idea is, the better it will have to be managed.

The creative moment, which is rated as so important, also tends to mask the down to earth quality of the actual work process.

I think creative people they are just like a doctor; they have to know what they are doing.

Mauro Alancar

Steve Simpson: »It's ultimately a fairly practical job that we do.«

The responsibility for the idea and making sure that it functions and works properly is therefore, neither artistic nor mystical. *Mauro Alancar: »I don't feel that we are any more special than anybody else. I think creative people they are just like a doctor; they have to know what they are doing.«*

What would make your thinking as an Advisor more creative, and as a Creative more advisory?

Work for Ideas instead of Money

Sometimes you have to protect an idea from your own need for comfort. If somebody in a creative profession places more value on things other than the Creative Idea, then they will also set other priorities during certain parts of the decision process. Then the priority will be money, a company car, or some other expression of prestige. These can get in your way.

Johan Gulbranson: »If you think about money, you are lost. You must have a very little car, not a very big house so you can lose all that without having any personal problems.« If you focus on

success and money you will very quickly lose the feeling for what is unconventional. *Javi Carro:* »**Don't become bourgeois because if you become comfortable you become less aggressive.**«

Don't become bourgeois because if you become comfortable you become less aggressive.

Javi Carro

Simon Waterfall: »**It takes a long time to understand, you would do this for nothing, you would do it just to carry on breathing.**«

Are you working for money or for a Great Idea?

Demand more Freedom instead of Money

In companies where it is difficult to do great work, money quickly becomes "compensation". But Top-Creatives always decide in favour of the idea.

Nick Worthington: »**Neither of us want to be Creative Directors, we don't want to be involved in meetings, we don't really want to get involved in the whole business side of that business. We just want to carry on doing the work ourselves and we want more freedom. Just to make mistakes and successes on our own terms really.**«

You've to be really excited about what you are doing, and if you're not, then you shouldn't be in the business.

Bob Moore

Freedom and the right to make mistakes allows for you to set your own standards. A good work environment at the beginning of your career helps you to define a very high standard on your work. *Bob Isherwood:* »**Get in early at a good agency when you can afford to work for nothing! And stay with the work, never think about the money because the money follows.**«

The energy that Top-Creatives get from their work is reward enough for many of them.

Bob Moore: »**You've to be really excited about what you are doing, and if you're not, then you shouldn't be in the business.**«

Would you also do your job for less money?

Trust your Team Partners 100 Per Cent or Change them

If you can't completely trust your partner, you will not be able to express all of your ideas unreservedly and, you will lose a lot of time just expressing yourself too politely and correctly. The thing is that uncontrolled and spontaneous impulses help to keep things in flow. *Jon Moore:* »**It takes a long time to develop a very good working relationship, because you have to get to the point with someone where you can tell them it stinks, let's move on and not spend 45 minutes talking about why it stinks, or how upset he is with you and all this stuff.**«

This kind of trust has to grow. *Dave Linne:* »**At the beginning of a partnership, you don't want to hurt the other's feeling. But if you can find a partner who you work great together with, even if neither one of you is the most talented person in the world, the two of you together will come up with better ideas. This is much better than if you put the two most talented people in the world together who don't hit it off.**«

Too much control and your own considerations are filters that hinder ideas and spontaneous expression. This is why some Top-Creatives start describing their ideas with: "This is the most stupid thing I have ever said, the craziest and most ridiculous idea that I could possibly imagine". In this way you protect yourself and your idea from criticism, because you yourself have already said it is crazy and ridiculous. *Steve Simpson: »I think that when you have a good relationship with a partner you are allowed to feel comfortable enough to say: this may be a really stupid idea, and say it anyway. It's a very fragile thing sometimes, coming up with ideas, sometimes the best ideas on the face of them are right on the edge of being really silly.«*

You have to get to the point with someone
where you can tell them it stinks, let's move on
and not spend 45 minutes talking about why it stinks.

Jon Moore

For this reason, it is important not to discard ideas too soon, because in particular the crazy, unusual ideas relax you and open the Creative Process for new, unusual ideas.

Ho much do you trust your partner?

Believe that You will get Better all the Time

Success comes with experience, Top-Creatives were not born as such either. *Rich Silverstein: »After thirty I got better, I was terrible before thirty, I wouldn't have even hired myself, I would have fired myself, I was terrible and it took some time.«*

With time you will learn to sail around the well known risks more consciously. *Simon Waterfall:* »*You know they exist and steer around them like great big icebergs, half of it is underwater, you know that and you avoid it a lot more easily.*«

Rich Silverstein

I was terrible before thirty, I wouldn't have even hired myself, I would have fired myself.

The experience will teach you to place more trust in the voice within you. And the more voices you are influencing, the more you have to listen to you own voice. *Paul Spencer:* »*I listened to the voice within me, and as soon as I found that voice, I suddenly had something that was uniquely valuable and that really guided me from then on. As long as I'm true to myself, I've got no problem. You have to know yourself, you have to know your voice.*«

What would be a courageous next step for your personal development?

Get Fired Early!

Protecting ideas also means protecting yourself by staying true to yourself. For this reason, many Top-Creatives have been fired at some time in their career. Often this is because they set higher standards for their work than the companies they were working for did. *John Hegarty:* »*It was a big agency. I got fired about 18 or 19 months after I got a job there. I think I got fired for being a pain in the arse really, which I probably was, but I really felt that what I was talking about and suggesting, was right. I was just 22. It's salutary to be fired actually, you have to sort of think do I believe in myself, have I done the right thing? Should I have shut up? So a good firing does you good. Don't get worried, all the best people have been fired at some point in their lives.*«

Some of the best Hot Shops came about because of a good firing. Being fired is nothing to be ashamed of. It is a kind of natural cleansing process that is meaningful for both parties, because the company feels just as unhappy with this strange being, as the strange being feels unhappy in the system. It is an experience, and the earlier you experience it, the better.

Dan Wieden: »If you get a chance to get fired, get fired early, because you know that if you can survive that, you don't lose the sense of yourself.«

If you get a chance to get fired,

Dan Wieden

get fired early.

Risk your job for Great Ideas. If the company is good, you will probably be promoted instead of being fired. And if not, you will get a new chance somewhere else. The sooner you get used to the idea that you could get fired the sooner you will learn to manage risks.

Which of your ideas is way beyond what your employer would regard as a justifiable risk?

How to Manifest a Magic Kiss:

Production

The production of the idea is dangerous because from now on the idea can no longer
be formed. At this point, time and money start to play an important role in manifesting the idea
to make it a permanent matter. It is risky because, up to now, everybody could see the idea differently.
With the production however, it become visually fixed for the first time. It loses its light status and
becomes a fact. Now you need skills that will continue the further processing with enthusiasm.

is really

dangerous

Felix de Castro

Produce the Idea and a Vision will Come True, won't it?

While many Creatives take a relaxed view of the production after they have sold the idea, for Top-Creatives it is the beginning of another critical work phase. Basic mistakes in the idea will be very difficult to correct at this stage and every change can be extremely expensive.

>*Production is really dangerous. It's where the idea loses its
ethereal state and becomes a material thing.*«
Felix de Castro

If you are too laid back in this phase, and do not focus your complete attention on getting the best execution, with the best material, and the best partners, you will run the risk of the idea sliding into mediocrity or of losing it altogether.

Shortened budgets, mediocre production partners, and lack of trust, can steal a lot of energy from the idea in this phase. Sometimes, the lack of relatively small amounts of money can lead to the fact that later a multi-million dollar campaign does not work effectively.

What's decisive at this point is the trust and mutual enthusiastic vision of the goal for all partners involved. This is the only way that the idea can still be decisively improved during the production phase.

Top-Creatives have a crystal clear vision of what it is they want.

In most cases creative work is teamwork. This means that several visions of different people participate in the result and the execution of the idea. This has advantages because the different thoughts and perspectives flow together. It can however, also happen that heated discussions distract you from the original idea and destroy it.

Only, when you have a clear vision of how the idea is to look later, are you able to defend this vision against other perceptions and influences.

Donna Weinheim: »*You have to be sure that you have the vision of what each of those things that you need to shoot is going to look like in your head, before you go do it. So you have to plan it, you're imagining all the different visuals you need to put together, to cut together, to make that happen.*«

A crystal clear vision of the idea allows you to quickly form a clear opinion in complex discussions. This is important, because several decisions will have to be made to manifest the energy of the idea at the highest possible level.

John Hegarty: »*If you have a vision for where this idea is going, then just hold on to that vision constantly. Always go back to how it started, where it started, what was the feeling you had when you had that idea. Lock yourself into that. That's like the radar beacon, that as the idea goes out, it keeps you on course. It is very easy to get deflected, but somebody else may not share your vision, although they like the idea, they see it in a completely different way. You have got to stay true to what the idea was, you must do that.*«

It is characteristic for Top-Creatives that they know exactly what they want. After all they have already seen the finished idea with their inner eye. *Xavi Garcias:* »*That's why I have a reputation in advertising in this country for being someone who knows exactly what he wants. I don't have any doubts, and I always ask for what I want, because I already saw it.*«

In order to find out if the production of your idea is taking place under the best possible and most trustworthy conditions, ask yourself the following questions:

☆ Have you got a crystal clear vision of what you want to produce and what the result is supposed to look like?

☆ Have you got the feeling that your production partner understands you completely and that he can even improve your vision of the idea?

☆ Were you able to infect your production partner with your enthusiasm in order to let the energy of the idea grow even more?

☆ Are you still open and flexible for improvements even though you have a clear vision?

☆ Do you believe you have the best partner in the world when it comes to his creativity and skilled handicrafts to manifest the idea?

If you can answer these questions with "yes", you will be able to manifest the idea at the highest possible level. Later, lots of people will have been part of it, or wanted to. Take it as a compliment because only you alone know who accompanied you on this difficult journey. Maybe it was a good process as well? With the following tips and questions you also have the opportunity in this last phase of craftsmanship to continue to hold and increase the energy of the idea.

Look for a Partner that Makes Your Ideas even Bigger

With demanding new ideas, obstacles have to be overcome that nobody had to deal with before. A fearful or conservative partner will then very quickly become a problem himself, not only with technical multimedia applications. *Lars Bastholm: »I think that the tech guys have to be creative as well. If they tell me we can't do this, I'll go to somebody else who will find out.«*

Kevin Drew Davis: »The best technical people are the people that add to it.« Enthusiasm and commitment can make up for lack of knowledge. *David Levy: »I would much rather work with someone who is less knowledgeable about the abstract technical stuff and at least having fun trying to create something that's cool.«*

The best technical people are the people that add to it.

Kevin Drew Davis

In order not to lose the energy of the idea in this final phase, it is very important to work with the perfect partner. *Katie Raye:* »**Just someone that absolutely loves what they do and is so excited to try and find a solution. Someone that doesn't say no, or if they do they have three other options for you.**«

Do you get at least three solution suggestions from your partner for every problem?

Let Your Partner Feel Your Enthusiasm

Your ability to enthuse others for your idea is a good test of whether your idea is a really good one. Is the original feeling of excitement still there? If you are not fascinated by the idea yourself, how do you expect to defend it emotionally and enthusiastically amongst numerous other partners? If you are not completely sure of your idea you will not be able to develop this passion.

John Hegarty: »**You have to enthuse the photographer. You have to enthuse the typographer. You have to enthuse the director and the actors. They have got to sense your enthusiasm for something. If they do, they will give you that extra bit of enthusiasm.**«

It is power and passion that generate the necessary extra energy in the production process in order to get a really brilliant execution of the idea. It is the same drive that played such an important role in the evaluation of the idea and that literally forces you to want to implement the idea.

What could increase your enthusiasm for the idea?

Feel if You Have the Right Production Partner

Everybody who is involved with the production of an idea can improve it or water it down. Along with rational criteria, Top-Creatives also trust in their own subjective feelings when choosing a production partner, something that no storyboard in the world, and no calculation can replace.

Mike Wells: »**When I first started to work on it, I had a sort of pre-production meeting with five photographers. I showed them the ads and then had a conversation with them. I picked the one who had the closest feel for what I wanted. He was saying all the right things and it was some-one I felt I could work with to get what I wanted.**«

It is only on this basis of trust that it is possible to improve the idea during production, as it was the case in the Pepsi commercial "Security Camera" from Don Schneider and Michael Patti. Instead of the original version that was sold to the client, where a coke driver secretly takes a Pepsi from the shelf under the eyes of a security camera, and is then caught by an old lady, during the production with Joe Pytka this ending was not seen as being really funny. Spontaneously a different ending was produced where the coke driver secretly pulls a can from the Pepsi fridge, which then unfortunately pours all of the cans in the fridge all over him.

Can your Production Partner improve the idea considerably?

Convey the Heart of the Idea

Before the production, the core, the essence of the idea that supplies the idea with energy must be understood. This understanding gives all of the production partners a clear orientation when they want to add their own creativity within the meaning of the idea.

Lode Schaeffer and *Erik Wünsch:* »**Be sure who you pick to execute your idea and make sure that this guy or woman sees the same opportunities in your idea as you do. Everyone, the client**

and the director and the photographer, should like the idea for the very same reason you like the idea.«

Everyone, the client and the director and the photographer, should like the idea for the very same reason you like the idea.

Lode Schaeffer and Erik Wünsch

This helps when the idea is in competition with the egos and interpretation of others. *Nick Worthington: »It's really easy for people to throw other stuff in and you've got to be able to deal with it really fast, you have got to be able to know whether it's right or wrong.«*

Can everybody in your team describe the core of the idea in one sentence?

Portray the Biggest Truth in the Execution of Your Idea

It is not always necessary to have to put on a huge production to be in touch with the core of the idea, sometimes the exact opposite can strengthen the authenticity of the idea. *Nick Worthington: »Sometimes you have a pencil drawing and you decide that's got so much vitality and life and says everything you want.«*

Sometimes you can even reduce the production budget as in "Washing Machines" for Levi's. *Nick Worthington: »These photos have got a rawness, they're just cut out roughly, but they have got all the information you need and a real great feeling. It cost five or six pounds to have the film processed and they were exactly right.«*

Sometimes you have a pencil drawing and you decide that's got so much vitality and life and says everything you want.

Nick Worthington

In advertising and what often seems like a perfect world, original documentation material is far more surprising and also more authentic, truer and as a result, more powerful. *Richard Flintham: »We thought wouldn't it be great to have snaps than a photographer, wouldn't that give a fresh look, just a completely un-advertising sort of feel.«*

What form would make your idea seem more true and more powerful?

Don't Produce the Idea too Perfectly

It is small "imperfections" that make things appear alive, personal and lovable. Just like our own character has small flaws, ideas, layouts, and productions can be made more admirable and livelier through small mistakes. This can also lead to generating more attention.

Alexandra Taylor quotes Miles Davis: *»Anything that's perfect, I don't like and that's what it's like art directing is for me. That if it's perfect it's slightly boring. If you had an oddity in an ad, an accident that is more exciting, that makes it more a stamp of your own.«*

In addition, perfection costs lots of time, money and a disproportionate amount of nerves. In this way, a Great Idea can generate part of its power from the freedom that arises from this liveliness.

What would make your perfect execution seem livelier?

Don't let Special Effects Compete with the Core Idea

In many print ads and commercials special effects steal the show. But a good production is not an end in itself, neither is a good Art Direction. It is a tool that has to make sure to give the idea the most amount of power.

David Levy: »It's easy to create something that is dizzy and flies around and spins because that's the easy part of it. The hard part is to have an idea behind it. So all the things that a computer can do often mask the fact that there is no idea behind it.«

Everything that you do must add to the idea
and not confuse it or loose it in any way.

Alexandra Taylor

This can also mean that an idea should not be pleasant to look at in the classical sense, because that would not suit what you are trying to communicate. This is important for all of those that look at ideas from an aesthetic point of view or as designer. *Alexandra Taylor: »Art direction will never be a great art direction if the idea is not there. I'm keeping true to the idea all the time. Everything that you do must add to the idea and not confuse it or lose it in any way.«*

What else could you leave out in order to focus the idea?

Communicate Critical Factors with an Idea

At the production briefing, the aim is to trigger images in the heads of your partners. This can lead to subjective perceptions and misunderstandings.

Donna Weinheim: »People have their own vision in their head, their own pictures, their own thoughts, so it is very subjective.«

For his reason, in the commercial "Boy in the bottle" in which a boy is sucked in to a bottle through a straw, the analogy of a vacuum cleaner was used, where you suck up first of all, then with a WHOMP you are sucked in. This description was important to present the production with a clear picture of our own inner perception.

With what comparisons could you describe critical production parts better?

Brief Your Production Partner on the End Result

Top-Creatives brief their production partners on what the observer should be feeling or thinking in the end, when they see the idea. This gives the production partners and photographers, directors and illustrators more freedom to bring their own creativity into play. They will be measured on the result.

Bob Moore: »We know what it feels, it's just a matter of getting that across. You work with a director to say 'This is how I envision this and this is what I want people to think when they walk away from the commercial'.«

This kind of result-briefing puts the production partner in a position where he can produce the idea in an even better form that can surpass your own vision.

Does your Production Briefing describe the desired effects of your idea?

194 Protect the Idea from Your Ego

At the latest, with the involvement of other "dominating" partners, it can happen that the idea is being remotely controlled. The projection of your own ego into the idea can therefore lead to a watering down of the Great Idea. *Don Schneider:* **»Most of what we see is garbage and one of the biggest reasons for that is there are too many egos.«**

Instead of what you want, the aim is far more to keep a clear vision that is always open for better execution alternatives of others. *Jack Mariucci:* **»I've seen writers and art directors fight on a set, I mean violent fights. Where ideas clash, egos usually clash.«**

There's one vision, and what you have to do is protect that vision and be the arbiter of what's going to change.

Don Schneider

Keeping the energy of the idea without placing your own ego in the foreground is particularly important at this point, because there are others who also have several desires and suggestions that they want to realise with your idea.

Don Schneider: **»There's one vision, and what you have to do is protect that vision and be the arbiter of what's going to change.«**

Do you already manage your idea independently of your ego?

IV. The World Needs Great Ideas

Are You Going to Change the World?

There can be many reasons why an idea does not come into the world. Maybe it's not wanted, it got lost in the process, or in the system. Regardless of what difficulties you may have when "managing ideas", be aware at all times: that you are part of this difficulty.

Overcoming yourself and your own fears and comfort zone in order to achieve something unusual is one of the greatest challenges in life. For this reason every successful Creative has one particular characteristic:

Bite!

Train this bite. Make it clear that you are not really happy with what you have got. Exert yourself and don't give up where others would be satisfied. And please don't expect that others will be happy about your persistence. It will probably bother most people.

This is one of the reasons why the first Big Idea is the hardest for many Creatives. For others it is the second one, in particular when the first one was merely coincidence. It is not always easy to repeat big successes or even to go beyond them, but if you want to set the right conditions for your success:

Start Today!

Don't wait for others and don't be discouraged if everything doesn't work out immediately. You can train your skills best by applying them. Don't dream about Great Ideas and better processes, bring them into the world. You will then be a source of inspiration for yourself, others and new ideas.

You will seldom need the perfect execution of a work method, but rather curiosity and the consistency to learn from your mistakes. It is the enthusiasm for the job that is infectious, the energy that jumps over and motivates you to do better. The suggestions from this book will provide you with good guidelines, but it is not a magic formula.

Find your own way of holding and managing the energy. You now know the most important factors.

I wish with all my heart that your Great Ideas will set an example for others and serve as a benchmark. Remember great craft-masters do not fall from the sky, but:

A Master is Someone who Started Earlier ...

Thoughts for the Next Generation

Work hard, have fun, and don't do stuff that
other people have already done.

Jon Matthews

If you don't have input, you can't have output, that's it.

Mauro Alancar

Be true to yourself, be honest, and know that
you have the resources within you to make things happen.

Juan Gallardo

Believe in what you are doing,
and always try to find the positive in anything.

Sean Nassy

Just be true to the work.

Mark Sandau

Don't be creative, be normal people.

P.J. Pereira

Open your eyes and open your mind.

Edwin Veelo

Don't be afraid to fail.

Simon Waterfall

Be humble enough to accept that you are

Milka Pogliani

not performing well so restart again.

Don't confuse style with substance.

John Hunt

Don't confuse technology with an idea.

Everyone has to find his or her own way.

Enrico Bonomini

Train the Strategies of the Top-Creatives

In order to demonstrate the thought-processes and work methods described in this book in practice, and to make them applicable for everybody in their daily work

Catch the Big Idea-Workshops

were developed. Each of these Workshops trains the Best Practices of international Top-Creatives in a few days.

Here you will get direct feedback on your work methods, and by using real case studies you will practice how to generate ideas more quickly and more effectively. You will learn through strategically correct and creatively unusual success stories, how you as the Creative, Copywriter, Art Director, Strategic Planner or Client can manage the Communication-Idea faster and more professionally.

Develop better ideas in the shortest possible time. You will train the necessary thought- and work-processes in small groups, in "Open" or "Company-internal" exclusive Workshops. Here you will learn how to:

☆ bring your idea to the point where it fascinates the consumer,
☆ develop an idea that is equally as unusual as it is effective,
☆ optimise your Creative Brief with a convincing Benefit-Design,
☆ evaluate your ideas and those of others professionally and develop them constructively,
☆ lead yourself and your team to Top Creative Performance,
☆ and many additional tricks and tips with which you can develop better ideas far more quickly.

Learn the thought- and work-processes of the Top-Creatives, because Great Ideas are also only a question of practice.

Bob Isherwood: »***If you want to be the best in the world, it really helps to work with other people who are.***«

If you are interested in an Open Workshop or an exclusive "Company-internal" Workshop please contact:

IdeaManagement®
Ralf Langwost
ralf.langwost@catchthebigidea.com

Holbeinstrasse 57
60596 Frankfurt/Germany

www.catchthebigidea.com   or   www.ideamanagement.com

Index of Keywords

All specifications before the star refer to the number of the tip, all the rest refer to the page number.

All specifications before the star refer to the number of the tip, all the rest refer to the page number.

All specifications before the star refer to the number of the tip, all the rest refer to the page number.

All specifications before the star refer to the number of the tip, all the rest refer to the page number.

All specifications before the star refer to the number of the tip, all the rest refer to the page number.